money for life

how to build financial security from firm foundations

helen baker

MAJO
STREE

MAJOR STREET

First published in 2025 by Major Street Publishing Pty Ltd
info@majorstreet.com.au | majorstreet.com.au

© Helen Baker 2025
The moral rights of the author have been asserted.

 A catalogue record for this book is available from the National Library of Australia

Printed book ISBN: 978-1-923186-27-9
Ebook ISBN: 978-1-923186-28-6

All rights reserved. Except as permitted under *The Australian Copyright Act 1968* (for example, a fair dealing for the purposes of study, research, criticism or review), no part of this book may be reproduced, stored in a retrieval system, communicated or transmitted in any form or by any means without prior written permission. All inquiries should be made to the publisher.

Cover design by Typography Studio
Internal design by Production Works

10 9 8 7 6 5 4 3 2 1

Disclaimer: The material in this publication is in the nature of general comment only, and neither purports nor intends to be advice. Readers should not act on the basis of any matter in this publication without considering (and if appropriate taking) professional advice with due regard to their own particular circumstances. The author and publisher expressly disclaim all and any liability to any person, whether a purchaser of this publication or not, in respect of anything and the consequences of anything done or omitted to be done by any such person in reliance, whether whole or partial, upon the whole or any part of the contents of this publication.

Contents

Preface		v

Part I: Building on solid foundations — 1

| Chapter 1 | Essential financial foundations | 3 |
| Chapter 2 | Your construction crew | 17 |

Part II: Why property? — 29

Chapter 3	Advantages of owning your own home	31
Chapter 4	The opportunity cost	41
Chapter 5	To occupy or to lease?	53

Part III: How to buy — 69

Chapter 6	Navigating property finance	71
Chapter 7	Going solo or joining forces?	88
Chapter 8	Buying property as an investment	100

Part IV: Property in retirement — 113

Chapter 9	Owners don't pay rent	115
Chapter 10	The do's and don'ts of downsizing	128
Chapter 11	The Bank of Mum and Dad	144

Part V: Beyond property   157

Chapter 12   Once you're gone   159

Afterword   173
About the author   178
References   179

Preface

Why did I write this book? Over the years, I have written several editions of my books *On Your Own Two Feet – The Essential Guide to Financial Independence for all Women* and *On Your Own Two Feet – Divorce*. These books were born from a desire to help as many women as possible avoid costly mistakes, take action and feel safe about their financial future – to get on their own two feet and stay there. For some readers, this means taking the first steps towards financial independence, either as they start out in life or rebuild after a significant life event. For others, it's about refining where they're at financially and exploring what they could do to improve things.

Many women have shared with me, 'I wish I'd read your book earlier', or 'I wish I had met you sooner'. I often wished the same. In the early years of being a financial adviser, I was able to help so many women secure that balance of getting their own home, paying off debt, building superannuation and maximising their position so they wouldn't have to rely solely on the Age Pension, which we know is nowhere near enough to have a nice retirement.

During these years, I have also worked with many women who are in a good position to be in a great position and those in a great position to be in an even greater position. I've helped them to achieve their goals and sleep well at night. I have also helped men and couples.

Unfortunately, following the Royal Commission into Misconduct in the Banking, Superannuation and Financial Services Industry, the cost of financial advice has risen significantly. Many people now find it difficult to afford, while advisers are uncomfortable charging fees that reflect the value of their services, fearing these may seem disproportionate or unreasonable. As a result, people seeking tailored advice are often turned away. For many, the consequence is that they are not in the financial position they could have been in. Books offer an affordable alternative, allowing people to invest a small amount of money to learn more and hopefully move forward.

Having spoken at events alongside representatives from organisations like Forgotten Women, I am now aware that (at time of writing) more than 40,000 women in Australia are living out of their cars. When I first wrote my books, these women were aged 65 and older. Now, they are as young as 55. Why are women – who have given their whole lives to raising children and caring for elderly parents and grandparents – forced to live in such conditions? Some are even in their 80s! The stories I have heard would move even the coldest heart to tears.

And it's not just older women. Homelessness affects youth, men of all ages, and everyday people, many of whom are now living in tent cities. This is a global problem.

I believe many people could avoid such hardship if they had access to knowledge – if they knew what they didn't know and acted sooner. My aim for this book is to help those who may not have access to a financial adviser, giving them the wisdom and knowledge they need to move forward.

Preface

Investing in property is not the only way to set yourself up for the future. In this book, I hope to show you how many 'silos' can work together to create one big, beautiful picture.

My goal is to motivate you to take meaningful steps to set yourself up for life and ensure you have money for whatever life looks like for you. One thing I've found is that everyone I've ever met has wanted a life that includes a roof over their head – a place where they can call home.

You only get one life, and I want you to experience your very best life. I hope reading this book plays a role in helping you achieve that life and empowers you to share what you've learned with others. Wishing you every success.

Cheers,

Helen

Note: Remember this book is no substitute for tailored financial advice specific to your own circumstances. I strongly advise that you seek professional advice before making any decisions after reading this book.

Part I
building on solid foundations

Chapter 1

Essential financial foundations

"It takes as much energy to wish as it does to plan."

Eleanor Roosevelt

Every house is only as strong as the foundations on which it is built. Strong foundations allow us to build big properties that stand the test of time and allow us to live comfortably – rain, hail or shine. The same is true of our financial health and wellbeing.

In fact, there is no point in buying property – or any type of investment – without first having robust financial foundations in place. Wobbly foundations are like a teetering house of cards, ready to give way at any moment.

In the very worst-case scenarios, I have seen people lose their homes, not because there was anything wrong with the property itself, but because their weak financial foundations gave way underneath them. They quite literally couldn't afford to keep a roof over their head. The effects – financially, mentally, physically and socially – can be devastating.

The point of telling you this is not to scare you by any means. Rather, I want to point out just how crucial it is to get your financial foundations strong – and keep them strong as life's journey runs its course.

Five financial foundations

So, what exactly are the financial foundations that we all need to live and thrive? Good question!

In essence, there are what I call the Five Foundations – each as important as the others and interconnected with one another in many ways.

Let's explore each one in detail to understand the role they play in delivering financial stability and independence.

1. Emergency fund

While we hope they never strike, it is a sad fact of life that emergencies can and do happen – often with little to no warning. Natural disasters, scams, relationship breakdowns, illnesses, accidents and injuries, redundancy, pandemics, the untimely death of a loved one… the list goes on.

Emergencies are stressful enough without the added uncertainty of how to pay for your (and your kids') next meal or where you will sleep that night, which is why the first foundation is an emergency fund.

This is money that is specifically set aside for a rainy day so that you don't need to raid your savings or run around trying to sell assets in a fire sale at a time when you are distracted and distraught. It should be easily accessible in a hurry. And crucially,

Essential financial foundations

it should be exclusively your own – a 'get out' fund should you ever need to leave, for example, an abusive situation.

How much is in your emergency fund is as unique as you are. Some people feel comfortable with $10,000 in the kitty. Others need more. And others still can get by on less.

As a general guide, I recommend having enough money set aside to cover your essential bills for six months. This safety net can significantly reduce the pressure of staying safe, fed and sheltered during an emergency, allowing you to focus on your longer term recovery.

2. Spending and investment plan

If you're anything like me, the word 'budget' sends a shiver down your spine (there it goes!). It's like a 'diet' – sapping all the tasty goodness out of life, reliant on willpower alone to see it through. It also only tells half of the story – what is (and is not) going in, but not what is happening in the bigger picture.

That is why when talking about money, I prefer the term 'spending and investment plan'. It provides a holistic view of our finances and how we are tracking towards our financial goals. And let's face it, we HAVE to spend money to live. So, it's better to track that spending and understand where it goes.

Your spending and investment plan should cover all your incomings (wages, investment returns, trust income, any inheritances and windfalls received) as well as all your outgoings. The latter gets divided into *essentials* (food, utilities, housing), *importants* (car, clothing, lifestyle) and *luxuries* (at some point, you'll want – and deserve! – to treat yourself, so it's better to have that cash already set aside than rack up debt on the credit card or use Buy Now, Pay Later (BNPL) schemes).

In my own spending and investment plan, I actually break things down even further into small pots, including:

- mortgage repayments (or rent if you don't currently own a property)
- bills (fixed commitments like groceries, utilities, insurances, car, gym membership and other regular bills)
- credit card repayments (paid off in full each month so that there is no interest accruing)
- pocket money (an allocated amount for fun things like eating out and entertainment)
- savings and investments
- holidays (essential to our wellbeing!)
- giving to others (even a little bit goes a long way).

Having this level of visibility over your money is really empowering. You can see exactly how much money is coming in and when. You can also track just how much you are spending at any given point in time and where that money is going – think about those unused subscriptions you completely forgot about, which have slowly but steadily eaten away at your savings!

Armed with all this information, you can quickly and easily make changes if needed to stay on track towards reaching your longer-term goals.

Remember, though, this isn't a set-and-forget document. Your plan needs to live and breathe with you.

So, every time something changes, be sure to update your plan as soon as possible so that you can see its impact on your bottom line in real time. You may receive a pay rise or an unexpected windfall, or you could be faced with a new expense (such as the arrival of another child or fur baby, the purchase of an investment property or the addition of another car).

3. Insurances

Most people tend to think of insurances as a financial drain. But consider them this way: insurances are back-up plans.

If you don't need them, great! Life is rosy, and you can enjoy the peace of mind of knowing you're covered should things change in the future. But, if you do need to fall back on them, you'll be mighty pleased to have them in place. And plenty of people do need to fall back on them. In 2022 alone, insurers in Australia paid out a staggering $36.5 billion in claims.

Having insurances can help you recover substantially faster from an unexpected loss, keep a roof over your head, and offset much of the out-of-pocket costs.

There are two key aspects to insurance: having enough coverage in the first place and ensuring that it remains fit for purpose.

It isn't enough to just pay your premiums every month/quarter/ year if they don't offer enough protection should you need to make a claim or don't cover your like-for-like replacement costs. Nor is it useful to pay for insurances that you don't actually need (a good example being maintaining pregnancy and maternity cover under your private health insurance once you have reached the stage of life where having more kids simply isn't possible).

Review your insurances regularly to make sure they are still fit for purpose and that they offer you value for money. For instance, you will likely get a better deal on your comprehensive third party (CPT) insurance if you shop around instead of simply paying the renewal notice from your existing provider. For things like home and contents insurance, consider how the high inflation of recent years has ballooned replacement costs, so you may now be woefully underinsured if you don't adjust the replacement values.

On the flip side, it often pays to get in early with insurances because you will be covered earlier in life when you have fewer assets and lower income to fall back on.

Not only that, some policies, such as health and life insurance, have age restrictions and financial penalties if you join later than recommended. For example, private health insurers may apply additional loadings or exclusions depending on the risk you present. As you age, options for cover decrease, and inclusions may shrink – even as premiums rise. For instance, certain superannuation funds may insure you for $250,000, but that amount reduces annually to maintain a consistent unit cost. Additionally, some insurers won't cover individuals over a certain age, such as 60, while others may decline coverage due to health issues or being deemed too high a risk by actuaries. This highlights the importance of securing policies earlier, when terms and conditions are typically more favourable.

When it comes to property specifically, there are a few types of insurance you'll want to explore, depending on your particular circumstances, such as:

- house and contents (for your home and everything in it)
- contents only (also known as renters insurance, which just covers furniture, etc.)
- landlord insurance (for investment properties, to cover damage to or theft from the property as well as loss of rent – effectively doubling as income protection insurance for your rental income).

As previously outlined, make sure that whatever policies you have cover the full replacement costs as they stand today, and review them regularly to see if you could be getting the same (or even better) cover for less money from the same or a different insurer.

4. Superannuation

Given that it is typically locked up until you retire, super-annuation often attracts a lower tax rate than the rest of your income and has many other tax benefits attached to it, making it a powerful tool for funding your retirement.

Sadly, though, many Australians don't give super much thought during their middle years. They set it up with their first job, then don't really think about it again until they hit 50 or so and begin thinking about retirement.

But, stop here to consider this point: it is YOUR money. So, by leaving it to its own devices and not making it work its hardest for you, the only person you're short-changing is your future self. Treat your superannuation like any other asset and regularly check in with it to keep it in tip-top shape.

Don't forget that some types of insurance – such as life, total and permanent disability and income protection – can be taken out within your super. While this means one less bill from your everyday finances, it does reduce your super balance. Some policies may offer more generous terms and conditions when taken out through superannuation than directly and, for others, vice versa. It's worth noting that trauma/critical illness insurance, which is often the most commonly claimed, must be funded from your cash flow outside of superannuation.

Generally, when it comes to the details of the policy, no two policies are exactly the same and, if one is significantly cheaper, that is a red flag. Always seek professional advice to avoid a mistake.

Looking after your super is even more important for women. Statistically, Australian women live 4.1 years longer than men. Yet various factors, including the gender pay gap (currently 21.7 per cent), mean we have less money in super. In short, we have to pay for more and do it with less.

Many women rationalise this by saying, 'It's OK, my partner has enough in super for us both' – only to be caught out when the relationship breaks down, their partner has done something wild with the funds/or done nothing, or their partner's health deteriorates, draining those funds more rapidly than planned.

Top three superannuation mistakes

Superannuation is a complex business, meaning there's lots of room to make mistakes. The biggest three I see people make again and again are:

1. **Consolidating unwisely.** You've probably seen the super fund ads claiming that merging multiple super accounts into one saves money. Sometimes that is true. But not if that money goes into a super fund with a higher fee or one delivering poorer returns. Also, insurances attached to super are automatically cancelled when a fund is closed – if you don't know this and prepare accordingly, you could find yourself with insufficient coverage or none at all.

2. **Forgoing tax benefits.** You may be eligible for tax breaks if you make additional contributions to your superannuation. There are benefits around voluntary and spousal contributions as well as downsizer contributions (putting a portion of the proceeds from the sale of the family home

into your super) and my favourite – the catch-up legislation. All of these can help your super balance to grow faster while simultaneously cutting your (or, for spouse contributions, your partner's) income tax bill. Then, if you are a low-income earner (such as during those years out of full-time work while you were raising kids and/or caring for elderly parents or in-laws), you may be eligible for the low-income super tax offset and government co-contributions – essentially free money from the government to help grow your super. By claiming none of these, you lose out on all those extra earnings your super could have made between now and retirement, plus all those extra tax dollars you've shelled out.

3. **Failing to nominate beneficiaries/eligible beneficiaries.** Think your will covers super? Think again. Superannuation is dealt with separately from your will. As such, if you don't nominate your beneficiaries within your super or fail to update them when your circumstances change (such as after a separation), your money may not go where you intended. That could quite literally mean your ex pocketing your hard-earned super while your current partner and kids get left out. In most cases, 'Mum' is not an eligible beneficiary.

Self-managed super funds

Self-managed super funds (SMSFs) are an alternative way of saving for your retirement from traditional retail or industry funds.

According to the Australian Taxation Office (ATO), there are (at time of writing) 616,400 SMSFs in existence, with 1,148,481 members and holding $932.9 billion worth of assets.

SMSFs are popular because they give you some additional choices over where and how your money is invested and allow you to directly invest in assets that retail funds typically don't, such as specific properties, commercial real estate, wine collections or vintage cars. This has led to many financial pundits spruiking SMSFs, particularly in connection with property investment.

However, before you rush out to set up an SMSF, there are some important factors to weigh up, as they are not suitable for everyone.

There are strict rules around SMSFs that you must obey or face stiff penalties. You will have substantial compliance and auditing costs to meet that should be factored into your calculations. And you typically need a sizeable super balance for these costs to be worthwhile and to meet borrowing criteria.

Remember that an SMSF is still superannuation, meaning you cannot access the money until you retire. And, if you purchase residential property through your SMSF, you are prohibited from occupying it personally. So, forget about any ideas you may have of using your super to buy a holiday home that you can rent out whenever you're not using it! Nor can it own the family home.

Business owners often like having an SMSF because they can use it to buy their business premises – their business then pays its rent to their own superannuation rather than to someone else. Under SMSF rules, the business must pay the going market rates, though – no freebies to help the business cash flow.

If you're considering an SMSF, it should be both strategic and add value to your financial goals. You also need to think carefully about who else is part of the SMSF. For example, are some members nearing retirement and needing to draw down funds, while others are still building the fund? What happens if a trustee develops dementia or becomes unable to manage their responsibilities? You need to think short and long term and plan for life changes before you commit to this structure.

5. Estate planning

First things first – yes, estate planning includes making your will, but it's far more than that.

Estate planning covers what happens after you're gone as well as how decisions are made over your healthcare, living arrangements and assets if you become seriously ill or incapacitated (think palliative care, stroke, dementia, brain injury from an accident and so on).

Who do you really want to call the shots for you? Would they do so in your best interests or their own? Would they even know what your wishes are if you haven't written them down? Even if you have verbally told your loved ones, they can easily forget amid the stress of you being in the hospital and the pressure of doctors demanding answers on the spot.

Your financial wellbeing – now and in retirement – rests on what you do today. As does the financial wellbeing of everyone who will benefit from your estate once you are gone. It pays to give this proper attention here and now while you have the capacity and clarity of mind to do so.

Factors to consider include:

- Your will, which should be updated after major life changes, such as marriage, separation, births, deaths, inheritances, major asset purchases, moving home, etc.
- Executor selection, which covers who your executor will be and whether you should have a secondary executor.
- Power of attorney/enduring power of attorney to delegate someone who can make legal, financial and medical decisions on your behalf.

- Advanced Health Directive (AHD), which is an outline of what (if any) medical treatments you want to receive in particular situations, such as if you are in a coma. This involves more than just 'switch me off' – think pain relief, hydration, resuscitation, medications, transfusions, transplants, etc.
- Letter of wishes, which is an outline of your views and hopes about non-financial matters, such as how you would like your children to be raised, if you are leaving funds with the intention of private schooling/university fees, or who will look after your pets, as well as instructions for your funeral arrangements.
- Testamentary trusts, which are tax-effective structures for managing inheritances that can provide asset security and protection against bankruptcy, that can also be used to release inheritances gradually (for instance, you may want to release some money for a child at age 17 to buy a car, 18 for tertiary education, 25 for a property deposit).
- Custodianship of underage children and provision for them.
- Tax effective structures for your beneficiaries to maximise how much they receive from their inheritance and minimise how much the ATO gets.
- Structures to keep the assets in the bloodline.

Your will (or your won't)

Various studies have suggested that up to 60 per cent of Australian adults don't have a will.

Of course, it makes no difference to you once you are gone. However, not having a will can have major ramifications for the loved ones you leave behind.

Settlement of your estate will likely be delayed, and you may need to go through the courts to determine who gets what. This may cause tensions between relatives, and people or charities you would have liked to support may receive nothing.

The emotional stress, costly legal fees, delays accessing money and possibly wasted taxes only add to their grief at your passing.

Please don't rely on a DIY will kit that you pick up at the post office or one of those dubious sites online. As the saying goes, you get what you pay for. And many people inadvertently make mistakes that invalidate their will, defeating the whole purpose.

Another point to make about wills: when you get married, your will becomes void. With so much going on at wedding time, it is so easy to overlook this. However, it warrants your attention to ensure that your will reflects your new reality as a newlywed – especially if this isn't your first marriage. You may also benefit from having a pre-nuptial agreement drawn up to protect your assets and any children from a previous relationship.

You don't know what you don't know

Money is a complex business. Really complex. This is why financial advisers, accountants and lawyers go through so much study to become – and stay – qualified. There is a lot to know, and the laws around tax, superannuation and financial affairs change all the time.

With that in mind, I cannot recommend strongly enough that you seek professional advice to get your financial foundations as strong as they can be. The costs of getting things wrong can far outweigh the fees of getting the right advice from the outset. Plus, you get to enjoy the peace of mind of knowing that your money is ticking along nicely, allowing you to focus your efforts on the next big thing – buying that property!

Chapter summary

- Financial security is built on five firm foundations: an emergency fund, a solid spending and investment plan, having insurance in place, contributing to superannuation, and estate planning.
- You must have a will in place and review it regularly.
- You don't know what you don't know, so seek financial advice.

Chapter 2

Your construction crew

*"Don't base your decisions on the advice of those
who don't have to deal with the results."*

Anonymous

In Chapter 1, we covered WHAT you need to do to build and maintain strong financial foundations. This chapter is devoted to exploring WHO you need on your team (your construction crew) to do that. While financial wellbeing and independence are about you, it really takes a team effort to achieve and sustain that state of being. Why? Because, as mentioned previously, you don't (and can't!) know absolutely everything there is to know about money, property, tax, etc. But you also don't know what you don't know.

Think about building a new house. No single person designs, builds and fits out the entire property. Each stage requires specific technical skills, industry qualifications and on-the-job experience to get the project done right.

Instead, a construction crew made up of a number of different specialists collaborates to deliver the completed property. The architect draws up the design plans; the excavator does the preparatory earthworks; the concreter lays the slab; the builder constructs the frame; the bricklayer lays the bricks, and so on. Some specialists play a one-off role, while others come and go throughout the entire project to work on particular aspects as needed.

Building wealth and financial independence works the same way. Each specialist plays a particular role in ensuring your overall situation is strong, secure and safe. And, importantly, they will also help you avoid making costly mistakes – particularly ones that may not become apparent until years later.

Who you need in your crew

No one team is the same. Each is made up of a number of individuals with their own unique talents and expertise. And each team is put together for a particular purpose.

Your team should be made up of people with the relevant expertise and current qualifications in the areas that are relevant to achieving your particular goals. They may need to be located in a specific geographic area for logistical purposes as well as having all-important local knowledge (given that one of the central considerations of property is location, location, location). Perhaps, most importantly, you have to feel comfortable working with them, giving them all the relevant information they need to make fully informed decisions, and trusting both the advice they provide and their commitment to you as a client for the long term.

They should also communicate their advice in clear, accessible language that you can understand. If you always need a dictionary or Google on hand to decipher what they're saying, they are probably not the right fit for you.

With that in mind, here is a look at some of the key people you may need to recruit to your team.

Financial adviser (also known as a financial planner)

Most financial advisers provide information about investments and insurance, but they should go way beyond that: they can take a holistic view of your income and assets, investment structures, superannuation, wealth creation, and risk mitigation options. They also cover tax strategies, retirement, redundancy, major life events, inheritances, divorce and estate planning, government benefits and pensions, debt management, and credit assistance. Remember that the job of a financial adviser is to provide tailored advice, not to sell you a product or service.

Accountant

Accountants are great at preparing your compliance work (think your tax return) and can determine the exact amount of capital gains tax/losses within a given financial year, so they can advise you on what to do and when. However, they can also give input to structural advice and prepare or outsource documents and deeds (e.g. trusts, companies and types of trusts) in conjunction with your financial adviser and lawyer. Remember that some accountants typically look in the rear-view mirror at what has already happened, but others are about planning for the future. You may need a business advisory specialist to help with forward-thinking tax strategies and structures. Accountants are strictly tax specialists – by law, they are not allowed to offer financial advice unless licensed to do so.

Bookkeeper

If you have a business, you may benefit from your accounts (and your regular Business Activity Statement or BAS) being sorted out by a bookkeeper, who then passes on the prepared paperwork to the accountant for high-level advice.

Mortgage/finance broker

The financial broker is your alternative to going to the bank or lender directly. They can source more loan choices and the best interest rates to organise your borrowing needs for your home, investments and business, as well as the structure of the loans. If you are borrowing, it is important to have sought financial advice first and for the broker and financial adviser (and often the accountant too) to work together to help you determine factors such as: Should your home loan have an offset account or be a line of credit? What name should you borrow in? What are the consequences of certain structures? The set-up may have costly consequences if it's not done with a vision for the future in mind. It's also important to seek advice about how much you are comfortable borrowing, as opposed to being told how much you can borrow and over-stretching yourself.

General insurance broker

General insurance brokers handle the insurance cover for your house, car, contents, pets, business premises, and landlord insurance. They will deal with public liability, public indemnity and other business-related insurances. Just as a mortgage/finance broker helps ensure your loans are good value, an insurance broker helps you to get the best value from insurances and ensures they are fit for purpose and offer complete coverage.

Lawyers

There are so many aspects of the law, and, like doctors, lawyers specialise in a particular area. You may find you deal with one firm for one legal requirement and a different firm for another. Some larger firms may cover various niches with different departments or have different specialists across a wide range of areas of the law. Of particular relevance to you may be estate planning lawyers, who prepare all the planning for you in relation to your estate, pre- and post-death wills, powers of attorney, letters of wishes, advanced health directives, various trusts, etc. Family lawyers deal with relationship issues such as family disputes, divorce, child access and negotiation of property settlements. Commercial lawyers handle general disputes, prepare business-related documents and check contracts. Personal injury lawyers are solicitors trying to secure a compensation payout for an injury.

Conveyancer/solicitor

Another area of law is property law. When buying or selling property, you will typically need the services of a property solicitor or a conveyancer to cover the legal transfer of ownership and related settlement processes. A property solicitor is a qualified lawyer who can act on all manner of property law matters across Australia, whereas a conveyancer is only licensed to act in property transactions and generally only in the state or territory where they are licensed.

Buyer's agent

As the name suggests, a buyer's agent acts on behalf of the buyer rather than the seller. They will scout for properties and negotiate on your behalf. In addition to the time and energy you can save by outsourcing the grunt work of finding a suitable property and negotiating an acceptable price, the benefits of using a buyer's agent include getting access to their professional networks and off-market properties. Since they inspect properties for a living, they also have a keen eye for identifying problems and defects.

Property manager

If you invest in property, you will likely want a property manager to manage it on your behalf. Property managers find new tenants, collect rent, manage simple maintenance issues, conduct inspections and ensure the property is being appropriately looked after by the tenants residing there.

Stockbroker

Stockbrokers specialise in picking and trading stocks and investing your money accordingly. It may be possible to find a stockbroker who specialises in a particular type of asset, such as property. A licensed financial adviser who understands your situation and how you should invest can help guide you as to whether you should be investing this way and give you alternatives to consider.

Life/investment coach

Investing or buying something as expensive as property just for the sake of it is not a wise financial decision – you need to understand why you are doing it and what you expect from it. For some people, a coach can be useful to help clarify your goals and expectations, allowing you to be more deliberate in where you park your money.

Licensed builder

If your property investments involve complex renovations, property development, knock-down rebuilds or adding a granny flat to your family home, you'll need a licensed builder to complete the work. Make sure they are reputable, registered with the relevant state/territory trades body, and fully insured for their services.

Medical/allied health and social care providers

You can't make good decisions if your health (physical AND mental) is poorly maintained. Who and how many specialists from this area you recruit to join your team is entirely up to you and your needs. You could include doctors, a psychologist/ counsellor, fitness or sports coach, physiotherapist, masseuse, social activity leads, naturopath, etc.

Costs vs benefits

Many people believe, 'I can save all this extra money by just doing it myself'. That's fine, provided you know what you are doing. However, when it comes to matters of money, no one knows what they are doing across every single facet of their affairs.

Having been a qualified financial adviser, I still rely on (and am grateful for the expertise of) an accountant to manage my tax affairs, an estate planning lawyer to oversee my will and estate matters, a finance broker to keep my loans in check, a general insurance broker plus any other expert as needed. They know the ins and outs of those areas, the ever-changing rules and requirements and related financial products and providers in far more detail than I ever could.

Generally speaking, the cost of paying for an adviser's time is tiny compared to the money that you could save from mistakes avoided and taxes/fees/interest overpaid, as well as opportunity costs avoided (such as missed investment opportunities and unclaimed revenues).

In the case of mortgage and insurance brokers, their services are typically free for you as their client (they are paid on commission by the loan/insurance provider). Other professionals will have differing fee structures, reflective of their level of experience and specialisation, and potentially where they are located (state/territory, metropolitan vs regional). The most common include:

- fixed fee for service – a set price for a particular service (e.g. property conveyancing, a basic will with an estate lawyer)
- hourly rate (e.g. lawyers)
- asset-based – a set percentage of your asset portfolio (e.g. for ongoing financial advice) or of the property you buy (e.g. for a buyer's agent)
- commission – a percentage of assets you sell (e.g. real estate agents, stockbrokers)
- project-specific invoice (e.g. builder).

Debt control

For most people who struggle to manage their debts, it wasn't a single major event that heaped a massive financial burden on their shoulders.

Rather, it was a cumulative effect – spending more than they earned, often over a number of years; poor oversight of their spending and repayment schedules; forgoing cash in favour of more convenient payment methods (which, for their convenience, come with hefty interest rates and usage charges) like credit cards and Buy Now, Pay Later (BNPL) schemes.

This is another reason why a good construction crew is so important in building financial security – they have the experience to recognise risks that lie ahead and how to avoid them, as well as expertise in helping break the debt trap if you have fallen in.

For instance, a financial adviser can help you to live within your means and ensure you are maximising your income opportunities beyond simply collecting a salary (such as pensions, investment returns and dividends, making insurance claims where relevant). An accountant can help you reduce your tax bills and, if you have unpaid or late taxes, negotiate a favourable payment plan with the tax office. A mortgage or finance broker can help ensure that debts you do take on are as cost-effective as possible, with the lowest possible interest rate and fee structure.

Your independence depends on theirs

Unfortunately, there are many advisers and specialists who aren't independent and impartial. They may be aligned to a particular corporate entity and so strongly advocate their products and services at the expense of others that may be more suitable or cost-effective for you.

Then there are those who push a particular agenda – property investment and SMSFs being two of the most common examples. While the claims about their benefits may be accurate in theory, they are not one-size-fits-all and may not be suitable for your particular needs and circumstances.

In recent years, the Australian Securities and Investments Commission (ASIC) has been cracking down on 'finfluencers' – people who discuss/promote financial products and services in the media, at events, in books or online without holding the required Australian Financial Services Licence (AFSL). These people went hard in spruiking a particular investment or financial product without being accredited to offer such advice and often failed to disclose the inducements or kickbacks they received in return for pushing them.

Even those nearest and dearest to you, while meaning well, can unwittingly muddy the waters for you. Their advice is based on their own experience of what did or did not work for them. But their circumstances are not the same as yours, so their advice isn't independent (not to mention they are also likely unqualified).

So, when choosing who to bring onto your team, ensure they are:

- independent – not aligned to any single financial product or entity
- unbiased – not a one-trick pony
- qualified – hold current qualifications in the field and are registered with the relevant regulatory or industry body
- experienced – they have worked in the particular area you are looking at (e.g. as an accountant with experience in property investment taxation, depreciation, etc.).

How to tell if your foundations are strong

When considering what we have covered in Chapters 1 and 2, it becomes clear that strong financial foundations are an important launching pad for building wealth and security.

Diligent attention needs to be paid across different areas and by different people. That is, financial health requires holistic and proactive oversight of all the working components.

Ultimately, your financial foundations should be good and strong if you:

- have addressed all of the Five Foundations covered in Chapter 1 (and avoided the common mistakes that I flagged)
- have a suitably qualified, experienced and reliable construction crew at your disposal who have provided input into your overall strategy, identified relevant opportunities and risks, and advised you of the best course(s) of action and appropriate risk mitigation strategies
- have examined the relevant risks involved, implemented strong strategies to minimise/manage those risks, as well as developed solid contingency plans in case the worst happens.

Once you have achieved this (I have yet to meet a new client who has!), don't think it's a case of set and forget. You have done the hard work in building strong foundations, but they need ongoing maintenance to ensure they stay strong.

Proactively monitor your foundations over time. If you notice cracks appearing, get to work on shoring them up as soon as you can. When your circumstances change (and they inevitably will change throughout life – with partnerships, children, relocations, jobs, deaths), update them accordingly. This is an important habit that will serve you for the rest of your days.

Chapter summary

- Invest in building a strong team of advisers around you.
- Ensure the advice you receive is independent.
- Keep your debt under control.
- Focus on the Five Foundations (Chapter 1).

Part II

why property?

Chapter 3

Advantages of owning your own home

"Home is a shelter from storms – all sorts of storms."
William J. Bennett

Having a home of your own (even with the help of a mortgage) offers so much more than just the ability to paint the walls any colour you like and hang pictures wherever you want (although, let's face it, being able to personalise our living space and 'nest' is a great source of comfort and pride).

Property ownership is the single biggest determinant of financial and physical stability, as well as quality of life in retirement. It is one of the ways to contribute to long-term wealth creation. There are other strategic methods, and then there are fingers-crossed methods such as creating the next Google or winning the Lotto but, let's face it, the odds of achieving either of those are very much stacked against us.

Let's take a look at where home ownership in Australia currently sits and why owning property matters for our current and future financial wellbeing.

Home ownership – facts and figures

At its very core, home ownership is about security: a stable and comfortable place for ourselves and our families to live, a safe place to store our essentials and treasured keepsakes, a retreat from the world to nurture ourselves and heal from the stresses of modern life.

It also doubles as a primary source of wealth creation. Residential property makes up 67.9 per cent of our total household wealth. So, when it comes to building financial security and being able to afford to live comfortably, owning property does more than savings, superannuation or any other investment ever could.

Sadly, fewer and fewer Australians are able to access the benefits of home ownership. Only two-thirds (66 per cent) of Australian households own their own home, either with or without a mortgage, while 31 per cent of households are renting. Twenty years ago, it was closer to three-quarters (71 per cent) of Australians who owned their own home.

Younger people have been disproportionately impacted by declining rates of home ownership. In 1971, 64 per cent of 30 to 34-year-olds owned their home; by 2021, it was just 50 per cent for this age group. And, believe it or not, half (50 per cent) of 25 to 29-year-olds owned their own home in 1971. Thirty years later, that had fallen to just one in three (36 per cent).

However, declining home ownership rates have affected virtually every age group. As the Australian Institute of Health and Welfare points out, 'Home ownership rates have also gradually decreased among people nearing retirement. Since 1996, home ownership rates for the 50 to 54 age group decreased by 8 percentage points over 25 years (from 80 per cent to 72 per cent).'

Then there are the people who have no home at all. According to the 2021 Census, 122,494 people were experiencing homelessness, with women disproportionately affected. The number of females experiencing homelessness soared 10.1 per cent from the previous Census in 2016, compared to a much smaller increase of 1.6 per cent among males.

Contrary to the stereotype of homelessness being an issue affecting youth, women aged 55 and over are the fastest-growing demographic when it comes to being homeless.

The power of leverage

Why is property ownership such a crucial part of building wealth? One word: leverage.

The equity that you build in a property over time becomes an asset in its own right, which you can leverage to reinvest and grow your wealth faster. It is a source of money you can invest with that doesn't involve tapping into your own savings or household spending. And because of the sums involved with property (we're talking hundreds of thousands or even millions of dollars), you have far more to play with than you ever would have through savings alone.

You can choose whether it makes more financial sense to buy your own home or an investment property (or both if you have the resources). They can be interchangeable – perhaps buying a cheaper investment property somewhere different from where you live allows you to get on the property market in the first instance. As it grows in value, you can leverage that equity to buy a home of your own – meaning your cash savings can go towards something else. Or it could be an investment now with a view to becoming your home when you retire.

Furthermore, banks are nicer to people who own property. They are more inclined to lend you money and let you borrow more if you already own a home. That may involve using the property as collateral to borrow against. Even if the property is completely separate from your new loan, the fact that you have successfully bought a property and maintained mortgage repayments gives you a more favourable credit rating.

Having better access to finance allows you to do so many things, from making other investments to buying a new car or starting a new business.

A source of income

Owning property can provide a reliable source of income, even if it's not strictly an investment property.

Think of how that unused space could be turned into extra money. For instance, you could rent out a spare room to a student or someone in need of a safe place to live (a particularly lucrative prospect given the current housing crisis and tight rental market!). Alternatively, you might rent out a room or the whole property on Airbnb while you are away on holidays or out of town for work (giving you some extra cash and deterring burglars by having someone living in the house even when you're not there). If you live near offices or a train station and car parking is in short supply, perhaps you could rent out your spare garage or carport to commuters.

Another benefit, besides the income, comes in the form of companionship for people who live alone. An empty house can be very lonely, so having someone to share it with benefits your wellbeing as well as your bank balance. For women in particular, having someone else living in the home can offer an added sense of security. Older people may also benefit from having assistance around the home with household chores, bringing in groceries, and so on, which they may otherwise need to pay someone for.

A word of caution: any income you earn needs to be declared to the ATO, and it's usually taxable. Renting out part of your home would also mean being liable for Capital Gains Tax (CGT) on that portion of the property. Since the legislation around this can vary and may change, it's a good idea to check with your accountant to understand what applies to your situation.

Also, be very careful about who you rent space to. I had one client who rented out her spare room to a man, only to wake up one night to find him standing in her bedroom while she was sleeping! Insisting upon reliable references and even police checks can be a good idea if you are renting space to a perfect stranger; otherwise, tap into your network for someone who can be vouched for – a friend, co-worker, or distant relative.

Tax-friendly asset

Given that property's core function is to provide physical shelter, it is treated differently for tax purposes than other types of assets and investments – often making it a more lucrative place to park your money.

While you will typically pay stamp duty (a type of tax) to a state and territory government when you purchase property, and land tax may be charged on vacant land, your home (known as your principal place of residence, or PPOR for short) is otherwise tax-free. That means when you eventually sell it, the proceeds are all yours – nothing goes to the tax office. Usually, any other investment or asset you sell attracts CGT on the profits you make, which is calculated at the same rate as your income tax.

When it's time to downsize from the family home, you can take advantage of a special provision called a downsizer contribution. This allows you to deposit a portion of the sale proceeds into your superannuation, offering significant tax savings. Money sitting in your bank account accrues interest, which is considered taxable income and charged at your income tax rate (up to 45 per cent). However, within your super, any interest or earnings generated are taxed at the much lower superannuation rate of 15 per cent.

Even investing in property has certain tax perks. You can claim a tax deduction for expenses associated with buying and maintaining an investment property – everything from the mortgage interest to repairs and renovations, property manager fees and landlord's insurance costs.

You may also have heard of negative gearing, which allows you to offset losses on an investment property against your other income – effectively lowering your tax bill. You then (hopefully) make a profit when it comes time to sell the property but have reduced how much tax you have had to pay in the meantime.

A more comfortable retirement

Government data has long shown major differences in the quality of life of retirees who own their homes compared to those who don't. There is a number of reasons for this.

First and foremost, the reason for this is simple maths. By retirement age, most people have paid off their mortgage. That saves a huge chunk of money from going towards housing each month. Renters, however, don't have the same luxury. To keep a roof over their heads, they have to continue paying rent week in and week out, and they are at the mercy of the rental market as to how much that rent costs.

Surprisingly, this fact is not taken into consideration in publicly available estimates of how much money you need to retire. These estimates typically assume that you own your home outright and, therefore, have no housing costs. So if you do rent – or if you still have a mortgage in retirement – you need to add thousands of dollars each month to your living expenses, meaning you'll either need a lot more money to retire on or have a lot less disposable cash from your retirement income.

The Australian publication *YourLifeChoices* breaks this down into dollar terms. According to its Retirement Affordability Index, affluent homeowner couples spend $232 per week on housing, while pensioner homeowners spend $137 per week –13 and 14 per cent of their total spending, respectively. In contrast, renters on the pension have to fork out $295 per week – a whopping 30 per cent of their total expenditure.

For singles, the difference is even more pronounced. Affluent homeowners spend $156 (16 per cent) on housing a week, while pensioner homeowners spend $115 (21 per cent). Renting pensioners, however, have to spend $204 per week on housing – 38 per cent of their total spending. That leaves far less money available for other necessities like heating, food and healthcare, not to mention luxuries like travel and entertainment.

Importantly, your own home is currently not counted for Centrelink purposes when determining your eligibility for the Age Pension. So, you could have a multi-million-dollar home and still qualify for the pension.

Then comes the customisation of your home. As we get older, the need for customisation increases. You may need to install a chair lift or internal elevator for a multi-storey house, handrails, wider doorways, make bathroom adjustments, add more cupboards at eye level, soft-close drawers and cupboards, easy-grip tapware, doorknobs may need to be replaced with handles, and you might need more accessible power points. There are numerous things you can do to maintain independence in the face of arthritis, mobility issues and health concerns. These are much faster and easier to implement in your own home than in a rental property, where permission is needed and can be denied.

Also, consider the equity in your home if you decide to sell and move closer to family, make your dream sea change or tree change, or become a grey nomad and travel the country – or the world. Having that money will offer you so many more opportunities than if you have to rely solely on your retirement income. Renters have no equity to draw on.

Home ownership can open up opportunities to explore the world in ways that are not readily available to renters. For example, a friend of mine from New Zealand was able to do a house swap and take their extended family to a fancy home in France while their own home was looked after by the French family. It offered both families a very different experience from living out of hotels and saved them considerable money on accommodation – allowing them to spend more on experiences, food and entertainment to make the most of their time abroad.

Safety and security

After considering money and comfort, it's important to look at the security that home ownership provides.

As a tenant, you're at the mercy of the landlord and the wider rental market. You could be forced to leave at relatively short notice if the landlord decides to sell the property, move in themselves, undertake substantial renovations, or look to knock down and rebuild. Their bank may repossess the property if they fall behind on their mortgage repayments and demand vacant possession. Alternatively, rent increases might outpace your ability to pay, meaning you can no longer afford to stay.

In such situations, you're left sacrificing your free time to join the hordes of other tenants inspecting properties in the hope of finding one within your budget. Then, you must submit your application and hope that you come up trumps – a process that can take weeks or even months.

Depending on your circumstances, you may face one rejection after another, as landlords prioritise tenants who are younger and still working, have higher incomes, are coupled, or don't have young kids and/or pets. (Anti-discrimination rules typically extend to tenants, but it is notoriously difficult to prove wrongdoing, especially in a tight rental market where landlords are spoiled for choice on who they rent to.)

If you are really unlucky, you may be bounced through this process multiple times in short succession. The financial costs of moving, not to mention the toll it takes on your health and wellbeing, can be serious. Not to mention the particular distress this can cause you or your partner if you develop dementia, and every day involves waking up in an unfamiliar setting.

Having a secure place to live is also particularly important for women, given the previously mentioned figures on homelessness. The Live Like Her Challenge works to support more than 40,000 women aged over 55 who are homeless – and that is just in Queensland. Many are forced to live out of their car or surf the couches of friends and family in a bid to escape violence, often at the hands of their current or former partner. Others have been left destitute from a messy divorce or their partner's premature and unexpected death.

Even having an investment property ensures you can keep a roof over your head in such situations as a fall-back option. You may only need to live there temporarily until your divorce settlement is finalised, but it will keep you from living on the streets and allow you to focus on recovering from the situation that put you there.

Chapter summary

- Owning your own home provides leverage to build further financial security.
- Your home can generate an income.
- The sale of your home is capital gains tax-free.
- Home ownership will provide you with a more comfortable retirement.

Chapter 4

The opportunity cost

"Diversification is a safety factor that is essential because we should be humble enough to admit we can be wrong."

John Templeton

When it came to writing this book, my intention was to help you understand the key role that property plays, not just in creating wealth but in building financial independence and security, especially later in life. Without at least one property to your name, you remain at the mercy of others to keep a roof over your head – whether that is a partner, family, government or the private rental market.

That said, I believe it's important to consider the wider context. No single asset or strategy is the ultimate solution to financial health, and this includes property. The risk of putting all your eggs in one basket is two-fold – you miss out on other opportunities for growth, and you lose everything if that investment is a wipeout.

So, while the previous chapter explored the various financial, logistical, and lifestyle advantages that come from owning your own home (not to mention those of investing in real estate), this chapter looks at the other side of the coin – the major opportunity costs that come from focusing on property over other types of investments and financial strategies.

Understanding both sides will help you to weigh up the various options and make an informed decision about what is best for *you* in your *current* circumstances (remembering that these are unique to each of us and also change over time).

Paying down debt

At face value, a property (usually) makes money while debt (always!) costs money – so why would you prioritise paying off debt?

First of all, paying down debt faster saves money by reducing the amount of interest you pay overall. It also ensures that debt doesn't spiral to unmanageable levels, where the interest being applied outstrips your ability to repay it.

Secondly, how much you can borrow to purchase a property directly depends on how much other debt you have. A lower borrowing capacity limits the quality and location of the properties you can afford, which in turn impacts their potential to appreciate in value and deliver financial returns for you.

Most people have some form of debt. The trick is how you manage that debt. Here are my general recommendations:

- Use cash instead of credit where possible to help you live within your means, stay connected to your spending and save on credit card transaction fees.
- If you do use a credit card, be diligent in paying it off in full each month before the due date. That way, you are paying zero interest.

- Avoid BNPL services like Afterpay and Zip Pay, which often have big late fees and charges if you miss a repayment.
- Consolidate multiple debts into one with a low interest rate (such as credit card debts and personal loans into your mortgage). This should reduce how much interest you have to pay while also giving you much better visibility over your debt since you only have to manage one repayment instead of many. You need to be aware that paying the amount for longer will likely mean more interest, so be disciplined to pay the extra down quickly.
- Talk to the ATO sooner rather than later if you are struggling to pay a tax debt. They can work out a more manageable repayment plan and may waive penalties if you are up-front about your situation.
- Only use repayment holidays on bank loans as a last resort to avoid repossession. Not making repayments will cause the interest to balloon rapidly.

Another important point when it comes to debt management is to seek help if you need it. Services like the National Debt Helpline (1800 007 007) can support you to get your finances back on track. Meanwhile, counselling services such as Lifeline (13 11 14) and Beyond Blue (1300 22 4636) can help you address the stress and anxiety associated with financial difficulties. If you meet the criteria, you may also be able to access your superannuation in times of hardship; however, the amount you can access is likely not enough to help you.

Paying off student debts

Student loans, including HECS-HELP, are a unique type of debt. Since they are repaid through withheld income, attract highly variable indexation instead of interest, and are subject to government regulation, they warrant a closer look.

The age-old question among many young or middle-aged people is, 'Should I pay off my student debt faster?'

Sadly, the government no longer offers a discount on additional repayments. However, the benefits are similar to paying down other debts: your student debt will accrue less indexation (like the nasty 7.1 per cent imposed in 2023) and, once paid off, it will free up more of your income to put into savings (like a property deposit) and investments.

Plus, you may increase your borrowing power when you want to go for a loan. Your mortgage broker can help you calculate your borrowing power with and without your HECS-HELP or other student debt.

If you are going to pay down some or all of your remaining student debt, be sure to do so BEFORE the indexation is applied in June each year.

Consider the various ways you can make repayments. Rather than dipping into your regular income or savings, you could negotiate with your current or new employer that they make additional contributions on your behalf in lieu of a pay rise or bonus, which would be taxed more. Alternatively, you could use cash from unexpected sources – tax returns, an inheritance, gifts and windfalls – since this money isn't part of your usual income and won't be missed much.

Putting more into super

Making additional contributions to superannuation is something that many people overlook, which can be a pretty costly mistake when it comes time to retire.

The opportunity cost

Here are some of the key benefits of making extra super contributions:

- The more that goes into super, the more you have locked away in your nest egg for retirement.
- That extra money should grow further, compounding over time (think back to your school days learning about compound interest). The earlier you make the contributions, the longer they have to compound.
- Superannuation contributions are typically taxed at 15 per cent, which is far lower than the tax rates applied to other types of income and investments.
- The government offers many other tax benefits to encourage people to make additional contributions into their super or even their spouse's super. So not only can you grow your retirement savings, but you may be able to reduce your current income tax as well.
- My favourite piece of legislation is catch-up legislation, which allows you to carry forward unused concessional contribution caps from the past five years. This can help you grow your super faster, provide a larger tax deduction, and ultimately increase your wealth. However, you have to meet the criteria.
- If you are on what is deemed to be a low or middle income, you may be eligible for government co-contributions. This means the government matches your contribution up to $500. It is effectively free money – what's not to love about that?

The true value of making additional contributions to your super will depend on your particular circumstances, what your cash flow is like, and which income tax band you sit within. Your financial adviser can help you work these out.

Be sure to make any contributions before the end of the financial year cut-off to claim the tax benefits sooner.

Case study – Victoria

Victoria (not her real name) came to see me many years ago. She had a reasonable income, didn't have high expenses and had excess cash flow. Victoria had gone through a divorce and wanted her own home, which she bought with a mortgage. We set up a strategy to build her superannuation in a tax-effective structure with appropriate investments for her age and for the medium-term. She benefitted from the tax deductions, and then created a 'pension' (an extension of superannuation that you can do once over the age of 60). She used some of those funds that could be withdrawn tax-free to target the mortgage with extra payments. This enabled Victoria to pay off the debt before retirement or use some of her 'bigger-than-it-would-have-been without contributing' superannuation to clear the debt at retirement. Victoria's property was in demand, so she later sold the house and moved to the coast to live happily ever after.

This strategy needs financial advice to manage all the elements and avoid a mistake. Factors to consider are age, access to superannuation, size of debt, size of super, health, the Five Foundations, etc.

Case study – Sheryl

Sheryl (not her real name) had been widowed and moved to Australia from a country without superannuation, so she was starting from scratch. Sheryl had a reasonable income and low expenses but may need to return to her home country for her elderly parents, so funds needed to be available. Sheryl preferred to make some sacrifices to ensure she had a house and didn't want to retire without one. Using similar strategies to Victoria, Sheryl was able to keep building her superannuation. However, due to her delayed start, her superannuation balance remained much lower than Victoria's. At 65, when Sheryl could access her superannuation while still working, she was fortunate that a recent boost in investment returns allowed her to clear her mortgage debt. Sheryl chose to keep working, both to rebuild her superannuation as much as possible and because she enjoyed the benefits of working. This approach should enable her to maintain her own home, qualify for the full Age Pension (as her superannuation remains below the threshold), and use her superannuation to supplement any gap between her spending needs and the Age Pension. It's important to be aware that Centrelink and Age Pension parameters and amounts may change over time, which could impact your circumstances – either favourably or unfavourably.

Building a sharemarket portfolio

Investing in individual shares or managed funds – a bundle of individual shares or exchange traded funds (ETFs) – is perhaps the most obvious alternative to buying property. You can buy shares or managed funds directly through the stock exchange or use a financial adviser or stockbroker.

Interestingly, people tend to approach shares with a different mindset than they do property. Who would sell their home for less than they paid for it unless they were forced to? No one. Yet, surprisingly, people do exactly this with shares. Often, it is the fear of loss – 'If I don't sell now, I could lose even more if the market keeps falling' – or they are more willing to take the hit in order to access that money for something else.

Fundamentally, it is the ease of access that drives this behaviour. You can sell stocks with the click of a button, but property takes weeks (at best) to prepare, market, sell and settle on. You can also divide up stocks and sell whatever portion you want, whereas you can't just sell one room of a property.

This accessibility can be a good thing if used wisely – you can sell out when stocks reach a lofty high and deliver you a healthy profit. Those returns can then be put to use elsewhere. Some people are even turning to this type of investment to help them build a deposit for a property when savings alone can't keep pace with house prices.

Alternatively, you can retain your share market investments and use the income, i.e. dividends, to further invest, pay down debt, support your lifestyle, or whatever the appropriate strategy is for that season in your life.

Another benefit of shares is that they are very low maintenance. There is no hassle of dealing with tenants, chasing overdue rents, expensive property repairs or the direct risk of your asset being wiped out by fire, flood, storm, etc.

Investing in a business you are building

Self-employment isn't for everyone – yet it is for a sizeable portion of the population. In 2022, it was estimated that around one in seven Australians (15.7 per cent) were self-employed.

The opportunity cost

Funding these businesses doesn't generally come easily or cheaply. And while the risks are great, the rewards of building a profitable business can be particularly lucrative.

Not everyone will become a billionaire through their business (although some have – just look at Atlassian co-founders Mike Cannon-Brookes and Scott Farquhar).

Some of Australia's most iconic brands are family-owned-and-operated businesses, having created income and employment for numerous relatives over multiple generations, including electronics retailer Bing Lee, Haigh's Chocolates and real estate giant Ray White.

Many, many other businesses of far smaller size and prominence also deliver healthy returns for their owners, which can be in the form of regular income and/or capital growth in an asset to sell.

Typically, you have more control over your own business than any other type of investment: you can't control the sharemarket, the property market or interest rates, but you can work hard and make strategic decisions for yourself.

Conversely, businesses can be a huge financial drain, especially in their early stages, when you are faced with set-up costs and little to no revenue is coming in. Many owners also make enormous personal sacrifices to prop up their businesses, which can leave them personally exposed if it ultimately fails. Not only is a failed business worthless, it cannot repay its owner's director's loans, unpaid wages and superannuation, operating expenses, etc.

If you or your SMSF owns the commercial premises that the business operates from, you have a double whammy to deal with: a failed business and an empty property that is losing money until a new tenant or buyer can be found which is typically a much longer process than for a residential property.

Many business owners do not pay themselves superannuation with the hope that they will sell their business to provide an income in retirement. Given technological advances, droughts, floods, and consumer behaviour, the value of their business may end up less than they need or even nothing. It is a massive risk to put all your eggs in one basket, and many former business owners have found themselves without a home and with little or no superannuation. Sometimes, their spouses were not even aware of this situation.

Furthermore, if you are the sole owner of the business, its value can be inextricably tied to you personally, making it difficult to extract the value you have built should you want to leave. Clients are used to dealing with you and may not want to stay with the business if you leave. Or there may be no one else who can pick up the reins and do exactly what you do.

Retaining family ownership of a business is also not necessarily straightforward. Can the older generation extract their share – either as a one-off payment or regular ongoing income – without impacting its ability to continue operating? Can the younger generations afford to buy out the older ones? Do they have the necessary skills to keep running it? Will customers and suppliers keep dealing with the business under its new ownership structure?

Checklist – costs vs benefits

Clearly, there is a lot to weigh up when deciding where best to direct your hard-earned money. Fundamental to this should be understanding your 'why' – the reason behind your actions. Is this an investment to make money? Is it a lifestyle factor? Is it for a sense of security? Is it to provide for yourself and your family?

The opportunity cost

Being very clear on what is driving you will guide you towards certain options and away from others, helping to narrow down your path.

Then, combined with the expertise of your team outlined in Chapter 2, you can use this checklist to assess and refine your options to find the best fit for your goals and circumstances:

- **Up-front costs:** How much is needed from the outset? This involves looking at purchase costs, any registration or transfer fees, whether stamp duty is applicable, any legal costs, etc.
- **Ongoing costs:** How much will you need to chip in on an ongoing basis? Consider things such as any loan/ debt repayments, maintenance expenses, compliance and accounting costs, management fees, etc.
- **Funding requirements:** How will you pay for it? Do you need a loan? Do you have enough in savings? Can you leverage equity from something else? What offers the best value for money?
- **Future returns:** What is actually in it for you? Be sure to weigh income versus capital growth and future cost savings.
- **Accessibility:** How liquid is each option? Can you access that money in a hurry if you find yourself desperate for cash?
- **Time:** How quickly can you implement each measure? How long will it be until you receive the returns?
- **Tax implications:** There are positives and negatives to compare, so consider both the tax liabilities attached as well as the relevant perks/tax minimisation opportunities in play.
- **Your current assets:** Take stock of what you already have. Do you already own property? Do you have money in

savings? Is your equity in your home, business or other asset ripe for reinvestment? This can help determine how best to diversify your investments and identify opportunities to pay for new ones that don't involve dipping into your everyday money.

- **Risk:** Look at the level of risk involved with each option and contrast that with your personal risk appetite (that is, how prepared you are to take big risks for big potential returns). If you have a partner/spouse, ensure that you are broadly aligned before making any decisions.

- **Lifestyle:** Take a good, hard look at your lifestyle and future plans as these can help you see whether something is a good (or bad) fit for you. For example, if you or your partner are about to leave the workforce, will a mortgage add undue stress? High-cost commitments, like IVF treatment or healthcare expenses, might limit your ability to lock away funds for the long term. Similarly, if you're nearing retirement, your ability to recoup any losses from high-risk investments is limited.

Chapter summary

- Home ownership is part of a broader financial plan with the goal of having money for life.
- Paying down debt is an essential component of your money for life strategy.
- Remember to make those extra super contributions.
- Put some eggs in an investment portfolio.
- Building a business can be profitable and rewarding.

Chapter 5

To occupy or to lease?

"Let your home be your mast and not your anchor."

Kahlil Gibran

If you've read up to this point, you've probably made the decision that, yes, purchasing a property is your goal and a feasible next step for building your financial independence. Go you!

The next big decision you'll need to make is how you plan to use that property – will you occupy it yourself or rent it out?

It is easy to default to home ownership. After all, you need somewhere to live, so why not buy somewhere to live? And what's not to love about having a place to call your own that you're free to decorate and do up to your own tastes and needs?

Don't let sentimentality cloud your judgement here, though. Buying property is a financial decision first and foremost. Regardless of whether you buy something to occupy or rent, the decision needs to be made on its financial merits, which includes taking a good look over factors such as affordability, maintenance, tax, lifestyle, logistics, protections and other relevant considerations.

Home ownership

The key to making the decision to buy a property to live in over one to use as an investment boils down to knowing your why: why do you want to own your own home? Why is this the best option for you right now?

We have already explored many of the advantages of owning your home in Chapter 3, from building long-term wealth by paying off your own mortgage instead of someone else's to the emotional and logistical stability it offers.

Not only that, owning your principal place of residence (PPOR) is likely the most tax-friendly investment you will ever have. Unlike interest on cash savings, shares, a business or even an investment property, your own home is tax-free (except for the stamp duty you pay when buying it – the rates for which differ depending on the state or territory it is in). There is currently still no Capital Gains Tax (CGT) applied when you sell it. And it does not preclude you from accessing the Age Pension in retirement either.

Home ownership also frees you from the constant moving costs every time a landlord decides to sell, redevelop, move into or otherwise make the property and your tenancy within it untenable.

Plus, don't underestimate the emotional stability that comes from owning your own home. Being able to put down roots, hang pictures and paint walls to your taste, make friends with neighbours and so on without the constant threat of being issued a few weeks' or months' notice to vacate is a powerful thing. Stability, familiarity and social connectivity are key ingredients to a healthy and stress-free life. In turn, good physical health means more focus and better decision-making about other aspects of your life, including your finances.

Each of us is driven by priorities when it comes to property ownership. For some, particularly younger people, the soaring rental prices in recent years may make buying a home the more affordable option. Others, such as survivors of domestic violence or those who have experienced homelessness, may prioritise the security and stability of having a roof over their heads above all else. Meanwhile, some are focused on minimising tax liabilities, finding a tax-free option too enticing to pass up.

Knowing your why is important because it will help formulate your approach, including:

- **The type of property you buy:** Will it be a house, unit or something in between? Consider the number of bedrooms and bathrooms, whether it has stairs or level access, and any special customisation requirements.

- **Where you buy:** Proximity to shops, schools and public transport is ideal for rentals but might not suit if you're looking for a home that offers complete privacy and solitude.

- **How you finance it:** Will you choose a fixed, variable or split loan? Will it be principal and interest or interest only? Are you opting for a 30-year mortgage or a shorter term with higher repayments? Will you need to pay for Lenders Mortgage Insurance (LMI)? (See Chapter 6 for more on finance.)

- **How it fits into your five financial foundations** (refer back to Chapter 1): Consider how repayments, insurances, rates and other ownership costs will fit into your spending and investment plan and what protections or contingencies you have in place.

- **Whether you set money aside for renovations:** Can you live with an outdated kitchen or bathroom for now? Would you sacrifice bedroom size to have built-in wardrobes installed?

- **Whether you diversify your investing activities beyond property:** Diversification is a good strategy. If your home ties up most of your funds in real estate, consider spreading your investments across other types of assets or shares in different industries to reduce risk.

- **How long you plan to hold the property:** For example, if you have kids in school, you're probably more likely to stay in the home long term compared to someone without kids or whose kids have already flown the nest.

All these points will, to some degree, be dependent on your age.

When buying a home in your 20s or 30s, you could easily still be living there 30 years later, with the mortgage likely paid off and the property typically worth many times what you paid for it. You're likely fit and healthy, can navigate stairs and narrow doors or passageways, and are capable of doing much of the minor maintenance and improvements yourself.

By contrast, buying a home around retirement age will be a very different experience. Much or all of the purchase price will need to come from the sale of your previous home and/or other savings/investments since most lenders won't look at issuing a 30-year loan (especially not for the majority of the property's value) when your working life is nearing or at its end. Single-level living is likely more important. A location close to services and healthcare will probably trump other factors. If you plan to travel in retirement, a home that is low-maintenance and secure enough to lock up and leave for extended periods at a time will be a high priority.

Remember, when it comes to mortgages, owner-occupier loans typically have lower interest rates but may offer less flexibility overall than investment loans. For example, not all lenders provide interest-only loans for owner-occupiers, and you cannot claim a tax deduction on the interest for these loans. If interest rates skyrocket to unaffordable levels, it may be more difficult to sell an investment property. Typically, you must sell with the fixed lease in place, which can deter buyers looking for a PPOR. They would either need to wait for the fixed lease to expire or offer significant financial incentives to encourage tenants to leave early.

If it is your PPOR, where will you live when you sell? You may want to consider whether to take out a bridging loan. Talk to your mortgage broker about options, risks, pros and cons attached to this strategy.

First-time buyers should also carefully consider the various grants, incentives and support schemes available, along with their eligibility criteria. Most states and territories offer some form of first home buyer grant or stamp duty relief, while the federal government oversees the First Home Super Saver scheme, which helps buyers save for a deposit. However, these programs come with strict eligibility conditions. You may be restricted to purchasing a new build and not an established property, only being able to buy up to a particular value or committing to living in the property yourself for a minimum period of time. If you are buying as a couple, it is unlikely that you will both be able to apply for grants and assistance on the same property – one of you will use it, and the other will likely forfeit their eligibility.

Case study – Lucy and Ben

Lucy and Ben, along with their young child, were trying to buy their first home. They wanted something fresh, new and affordable, so they ventured further afield to a new development quite a long way out. Lucy had to commute to the city for work, and Ben worked in the suburbs, but they needed two cars because of their work schedules and the location. There was no public transport close to this development, so they would always have to drive – to work, the train station, or the bus terminal. When they factored in the time for public transport to reach the city, it was significant. Living far out meant long journeys, and they had to allow extra time for traffic jams, incidents, or the occasional delays in public transport. Coupled with the cost of transport, they decided driving was still the best option. However, the massive increase in petrol prices, regular repairs and maintenance for the cars, and the possible need to upgrade one car for safety added more challenges. Upgrading a car would mean taking on more debt, which usually comes at a higher interest rate than a mortgage. On top of that, the cost of extending childcare hours due to long commutes added further strain to their budget. After only a couple of years, they decided to sell and move closer to the city.

When considering buying a home further out, remember to look beyond just the purchase price. Take the time to consider all these variables carefully before committing. Council rates and water bills can vary significantly – some areas might offer savings, while others might not. These costs should be carefully factored into your decision.

Time is also a crucial consideration. Long commutes can be stressful, which often leads to other challenges. Stress can result in time off work or reduced performance. Extended commutes might also mean missing out on important family moments, like kids' sports or school events, because it's simply not possible to get back in time.

The strain of long commutes can also affect relationships. When both partners are exhausted, arguments and tension can arise. Over time, this can lead to bigger issues, including relationship breakdowns. In those cases, the house may ultimately need to be sold, with assets you worked hard to acquire and made sacrifices for being divided.

The financial impact of moving again should not be underestimated. Stamp duty on the next house, sale costs on the current one, and the stamp duty you already paid on the first property can quickly add up. In new developments, property values may not see significant growth in a short time frame, which can leave you financially worse off.

Property investment

While we'll look into the processes and intricacies of buying property as an investment in more detail in Chapter 8, I want to give you an overview here of some of the things to consider when deciding whether this is the option for you instead of buying a home for yourself.

Property investors are often thought of as being multi-millionaires with a large portfolio of properties, greedily extracting every cent they can from their tenants. While that may be true of some investors, the reality is that most investors have just a small holding. In fact, an analysis of ATO figures found that 71.48 per cent of investors own just a single investment property, and a further 18.86 per cent own two investment properties. That has not changed much in recent years either – in 2017, well before the COVID-19 pandemic, the Reserve Bank estimated around 70 per cent of investors owned a single property. This is why the term 'mum and dad investors' has been used so widely – because the majority of property investors in Australia are small-scale. They are simply trying to get ahead in life and provide for their families as best they can.

Just like with home ownership, knowing why you want to invest in property is important from the outset. 'To make money' is not a good enough answer here; that is true of every investor. Dig deeper: there are many reasons why people invest in property.

For some, it is their only means of getting that first foot onto the property ladder – without the contribution of rental payments towards the mortgage, they simply cannot afford to buy a property. This is often known as 'rentvesting', where someone buys an investment property, typically in a cheaper market on the suburban fringe of a city or in a regional area, and then rents where they actually want to live.

Some people even make property investments their full-time job. 'Flippers' will buy a run-down property and give it a relatively rapid makeover before putting it back on the market with the aim of 'flipping it' for a quick profit. Typically, this is done on repeat, reinvesting the proceeds of one sale towards the next purchase. The ATO is clued up on this form of income and may require you to do so as a business under your own Australian Business Number (ABN) and potentially be registered for GST.

Elsewhere, private and amateur developers may explore land banking – buying up vacant land or larger blocks suitable for subdivision and redevelopment to turn a profit once a Development Application (DA) is approved or a more profitable change in zoning is implemented. Both of these options are high-cost (with up-front buying costs and stamp duty, renovation costs, surveyor fees, DA expenses, council rates, sale expenses, etc.) and not without substantial risk (chiefly that your renovation/ development timeframe and budget suffer unforeseen blowouts, or that the property market enters a downturn when you are ready to sell, meaning you face the prospect of selling at a loss or incurring additional holding costs until such time as you can sell for a profit). Both typically attract CGT on your profits, which also needs to be calculated in your financial plan.

Land banking is generally used in locations where you can't afford to buy land and a house just yet but want to secure that location for the future. Perhaps you are waiting for access to superannuation or an inheritance, or it is just part of your long-term plan.

Other people specifically look at ways to invest ethically and view property investing not only as a way to derive income for themselves but also as a means of providing other people with one of life's necessities – shelter. This may be investing in social and affordable housing projects. Alternatively, some people purchase property in areas where short-term rentals dominate the market, limiting rental options for locals, including essential workers. In doing so, these investors are willing to accept less rental income overall than they could achieve by using the property as a short-term rental to provide much-needed housing for locals. It is still an investment, though, and they still derive regular income and can also leverage longer term capital growth as the property's value increases over time.

Perhaps the biggest driving factor for investing in property is its perceived safety:

- **Property is tangible:** You can physically touch it, and unlike other investments, it cannot simply disappear due to a computer glitch or market crash. Both the sharemarket and property can be great long-term investment options, offering potential for capital growth and income. While property is often seen as a reliable investment, outperforming cash savings or softer investment options, it's not entirely foolproof. Natural disasters, like earthquakes, can result in significant loss, and there are situations where insurance may not fully cover the damage or loss. It's important to consider these risks when assessing property as an investment.

- **Property provides a basic need:** Shelter is a fundamental human necessity, alongside food, air and water. This ensures there will always be demand for it.
- **Historically strong returns:** Property has been one of the most reliable drivers of wealth creation, delivering great financial returns over the long term. (Note: past performance is not an indicator of future performance; there are no guarantees, and legislation and economies can change.)
- **Finite supply:** Land is a limited resource, which supports its long-term value.

The more people fear losing their hard-earned money, the more they gravitate towards investments perceived as a safe and reliable option.

Blended

Another option is to blend your personal use of the property with income-generating use by others. This can occur simultaneously or alternate over different periods.

Following are some examples of how a property might be used in a blended way during your ownership.

Converting your home into a rental property

Perhaps you decide to upgrade to a larger home but are financially able to keep your original property as well. Alternatively, you may embark on a sea change, tree change, or move interstate or overseas, choosing to retain your original home as a backup in case things don't go as planned. Or, if you're going on an extended holiday, you might decide to rent out the property to generate income to cover the mortgage while also ensuring it isn't left vacant for an extended period.

Moving into your own rental property

Some people buy a property specifically with the aim of moving into it longer term, such as in retirement, and rent it out in the meantime to help cover the mortgage repayments. For others, a rental property can become a fallback option to avoid homelessness, such as if a natural disaster wipes out the family home or a relationship breakdown leaves them with no money until a settlement is reached.

A holiday home that you rent out when you are not using it

It generally makes financial sense to derive some income from a property that would otherwise sit empty for most of the year. This can be particularly lucrative during peak holiday seasons (e.g. summer for beachside locations and winter for high-altitude areas that receive snowfall) and properties that are close to tourist attractions or in towns that host major sporting activities or cultural festivals.

A rented granny flat on your property

If you have a granny flat or space to build one (subject to the rules of your state or territory and local council), this can be a good option to bring in extra cash to help pay off your mortgage. This is a particularly valuable option for anyone who is what we call 'asset-rich, cash-poor', meaning they own a valuable asset (the property) but have limited disposable income. Any property that is to be rented, including a granny flat, typically needs to meet certain requirements, such as having its own entrance (not through your own home), being fitted with smoke detectors, and meeting minimum ceiling heights (many converted under-house areas do not meet this standard). You may also need to fence off the granny flat to divide it from your own home to make it more attractive to prospective tenants and also more private for you and your family. Alternatively, if money is really tight or you are now living alone, you could move into the granny flat yourself and rent out the main house!

Buying a home to subdivide or redevelop

In some cases, it is not the house itself that has the potential for blended usage but the land it sits on. Larger blocks may be suitable for subdivision if you have the patience to work through the council approvals process and any rezoning requirements, allowing you full and uninterrupted use of the house and selling off a portion of the land. Alternatively, older homes can be ripe for a knockdown-rebuild, which may present the opportunity to add an investment component, such as building a granny flat to rent out or a duplex where you can move into one side and rent out or sell the other.

Flipping your home

As already outlined, flipping can be a profitable investment strategy. However, if you live in the property while undertaking the renovations, you generally need to do so for a minimum period of time for the ATO to consider it your PPOR rather than an investment. This classification can exempt you from CGT when you sell the property. Additionally, there may be restrictions on how many times you can use this exemption as an owner-occupier for tax purposes.

A word of caution on blended property

Given the merging of uses, the lines become very blurred for tax purposes, meaning good record-keeping and a proficient accountant are essential – otherwise, you risk falling afoul of the ATO and incurring hefty tax bills with interest and penalties, or going the other way and missing out on claiming legitimate deductions.

What those records involve will depend on how you blend your personal use of the property with income-generating activities. Remember that CGT will typically be applied when you sell the property, but only for the period(s) where you were generating income from it, and you cannot claim tax deductions for property-related expenses while you are using the property. Any holiday home that you rent out while you are not using it can be more difficult to track, given the comings and goings throughout the year and the constant switching between it being your own property and an income-generating one.

Documents like rental agreements, property management contracts, holiday booking receipts and visitor logbooks for short-term or holiday rentals (which is also handy to have for insurance purposes should you ever need to make a claim) are useful records to keep, showing what the property was used for and when.

Regardless of what you do, keeping receipts is essential for proving what you paid for and when. However, simply stacking them in a shoe box is not the best idea – those shiny paper receipts quickly fade, rendering them useless; there's also no organisation or clear context about the expense and individual receipts are easily lost. A better approach is to use a digital solution to store your receipts. There are many apps available to help you do this, which are becoming increasingly sophisticated, meaning your input can be as simple as taking a photo of the receipt using your mobile phone as soon as you receive it. Job done!

Another consideration is that your financing arrangements will likely need to change as the property's usage changes. For example, your home loan agreement may specifically preclude you from renting out the property, meaning you will need to refinance it to an investment loan, which typically has a higher interest rate and may involve loan transfer fees. If you are going the other way and making a rental property your own home, you definitely should look to refinance to an owner-occupier mortgage as soon as possible to get that interest rate down.

Insurances will also need to be revisited to ensure they are fit for purpose and that you are fully covered. Many home insurance policies specifically prohibit you from using the property for income-generating activities. Should you ever need to make a claim, you may find that you are not actually covered if you have rented out the property or even used it for a home-based business. You should also be aware that if you have claimed rent and costs for a home-based business, you may be liable for a portion of capital gains tax.

Chapter summary

- Whether to buy a property to live in or to lease depends on your 'why' and, to a great extent, your age.
- There are blended options that allow you to be an owner and a landlord.
- Any investment activity must be supported by sound record-keeping and insurances in case things go awry.

Part III
how to buy

Chapter 6

Navigating property finance

"Price is what you pay. Value is what you get."

Warren Buffett

Buying property is the single biggest financial commitment most of us ever make in our lifetimes. The numbers we're dealing with are obviously very large, so mistakes here can be costly indeed. And because property finance is such a complex area, the scope for making mistakes is huge.

How much you borrow, from whom, for how long and under what terms can quite literally make a difference of hundreds of thousands of dollars over the life of the loan. This is also where discipline plays a key role. It is very easy to keep topping up borrowings for holidays, cars, etc., but you are generally paying this loan for 30 years, so the interest will far exceed the value of a depreciating asset, such as a car or holiday.

This also applies to constantly refinancing, which not only involves upfront costs but also extends the loan term, resulting in more interest paid and less net wealth over time.

While refinancing may sometimes be necessary, go in with your eyes wide open. Interest on large borrowings adds up significantly over many years. Consider your priorities: would you prefer to pay off your home loan sooner, giving yourself options like early retirement, reduced work hours or a year off work, or is it more important to have things now and work longer to afford them?

I can't emphasise enough just how important it is for you to be crystal clear about what you are getting into and what it will ultimately cost you in the long term before you sign on the dotted line, which is why this chapter is specifically dedicated to all things property finance.

Choosing the right lender

Mention the word 'mortgage' or 'loan' and most people tend to think of one of the big four banks: ANZ, Commonwealth Bank, National Australia Bank or Westpac. In fact, in May 2024, comparison website Canstar estimated that 73 per cent of all owner-occupier home loans in Australia are with the big four.

Why do so many people borrow from the big four? There are numerous reasons. It could be because of their size they are viewed as a safer option, or because they are the most recognisable. Some borrowers prefer having access to a branch network to deal with the bank in person instead of being confined to dealing with their lender online or over the phone. The convenience of integrating loans with everyday banking is another driving factor.

The big four banks are far from the only options, though. Smaller banks, credit unions, online lenders, and non-bank lenders (that is, ones that specialise in offering credit, such as loans, but do not offer other banking services like accounts and term deposits) are among the other options available to you.

Smaller lenders obviously don't have the size and branch network of the big four, which can be both a good and a bad thing.

Accessing customer support may be more difficult when you can't simply walk into a branch at your local shopping or town centre. Smaller lenders also have to be more cautious about who they lend to, so they tend to be more risk-averse and turn away prospective borrowers they don't feel comfortable dealing with. In some cases, only the big four are willing to lend.

On the flip side, without the high costs of maintaining such a network of branches (including retail rents, staff, energy costs, etc.), these lenders can afford to offer better deals to their customers in the form of lower interest rates and cheaper fees. Often, there is less (or even no) time waiting in awful phone queues for hours and navigating automated prompts when you need support. Many also specialise in lending to particular types of borrowers, such as those who are self-employed or have particular loan requirements that are too niche for the big four to consider.

There are several major factors to beware of when weighing up which lender to go with.

Firstly, watch out for the loyalty tax. Just because you have banked with a particular lender for years doesn't mean they will automatically give you the best deal. In fact, the reverse is often true – lenders offer lucrative discounted interest rates and/or waive fees to new customers while lumping existing customers with more expensive rates and high-fee options.

Secondly, don't go applying to various lenders to see what offers you get. Every loan application you make is recorded on your personal credit score. Too many applications can adversely affect your credit rating, which in turn can cause lenders to avoid you like the plague or charge you more than someone else borrowing the same amount who only made one application.

Finally, be really diligent in looking over the details within a loan agreement before signing. Every lender has its own terms and conditions, fees and charges, so weigh them up carefully when comparing your options.

For instance, there may be expensive fees for terminating the loan (such as if you refinance to another lender or sell the property) within a particular time period or if you pay off the loan early. Some lenders charge additional fees for related loan products, such as offset accounts or credit cards. Try to negotiate these fees to be waived or look for options that don't charge them at all. If you do accept them, make sure that you will pay them directly instead of having them automatically rolled into your loan, where they will accrue interest.

Rate considerations

The most obvious factor to look at when weighing up mortgage options is, naturally, the interest rate you'll be paying.

We will explore variable and fixed interest rates, along with other aspects, in more detail shortly. For now, keep these main points in mind:

- Pay close attention to the details.
- Interest rates are often negotiable, at least to some extent.

Most lenders have what they call a 'headline rate', which is the standard interest rate they offer. However, many offer new customers a discount on this rate to entice them in. Don't be fooled into thinking this discount rate is what you will be paying in the long term – most are only introductory rates, which last for just a few months to a year. After this introductory period, the discount disappears and the interest rate charged automatically defaults to the headline rate. Depending on the size of the discount that was offered, this can be quite a rude shock to borrowers whose repayments suddenly increase markedly. If you haven't budgeted for this increase, your everyday finances will quickly feel the pinch, and you may start to fall behind on your repayments.

You may also be shocked to discover that interest rates are negotiable – you are perfectly within your rights to haggle for a better rate. This applies both to when taking out a new loan and refinancing an existing one. If the lender REALLY wants your business, it will engage with you and negotiate a more favourable rate for you, which could slash half a percentage point (or more!) off your rate.

Half a per cent may not sound like much but let me put that into context. Say you secure a 0.5 per cent discount off a 6 per cent rate for a $400,000 mortgage. Over 30 years (the standard term for a mortgage), you would save more than $41,600 in interest! Clearly, it pays to ask. And if you don't ask, you won't get – lenders aren't in the habit of handing out big discounts freely.

When negotiating rates, use your unique bargaining power to your advantage. Lenders will be more open to negotiating with you and offering bigger discounts if you have a loan-to-value ratio (LVR) below 80 per cent, have a good credit rating, do not have any other debts, have been in your current job for longer than six months or have a stable employment history in the same industry, or have what they deem to be a high-value loan (this figure will vary across lenders, but typically loans above $700,000 to $1 million are considered to be high value).

The value of a mortgage broker

Over the many years I have worked with clients and their mortgage broker (and sometimes also the accountant and estate planner to make sure the left and right hands are working together), I've seen firsthand the benefits of having a quality mortgage broker as part of your team. In my experience, a skilled broker brings more planning and options to the table.

For example, take Katie, who owned her own home but wasn't happy there. We pulled in a mortgage broker to help Katie explore several options, including:

- whether to sell the current property and buy elsewhere
- whether to keep the current property as an investment property and rent it out, and determine how much Katie could borrow, could afford to borrow and would feel comfortable borrowing
- whether to buy another property and invest in other investments like shares/managed funds
- cashflow considerations under each scenario
- the amount of interest paid under these scenarios
- how her overall wealth might look in a set number of years
- structuring options, such as using offset accounts, choosing between principal-and-interest (P&I) or interest-only (IO) loans, and deciding whose name the purchase should be made in.

By working with a broker, we could explore a range of options and make informed decisions beyond just focusing on interest rates. This provides a more holistic approach for clients. For example, a broker can help determine whether and how to restructure loans to shift from non-tax-deductible debt to tax-deductible debt.

In contrast, individual banks are limited to recommending only their own products. Mortgage brokers, however, can compare a range of lenders, present their rates and terms, and help you weigh the pros and cons of each option. They often advocate for you and help you through the loan process. Before you start seriously looking at a property, a good broker can prepare you in advance and assess how your financial situation needs to look to get a loan approved easily, such as if you have a bad credit history, need to look at other options like private lenders or consider schemes such as first home buyers grants. Good brokers, familiar with the different policies and criteria of various lenders, can quickly rule out unsuitable lenders and save you time and angst from the beginning of the process.

Generally, mortgage brokers are paid a commission by the lender for the loan, and this does not come at the client's expense. However, in some cases, a broker may charge a fee – such as when their work helps you secure a better deal with your current bank or provides you with a clearer understanding of your options. A fee may also apply where your particular situation is more complex in nature. If so, the broker should disclose this upfront. If the property in question is an investment property, you should talk to your accountant about whether the broker's fee is tax deductible.

According to a mortgage broker friend, the 5 Cs that help you get a great deal are:

- credit history
- character
- capacity
- collateral
- conditions.

Planning is key, and having your team support you through the process will help you make an informed decision about all aspects of this journey, give you confidence, and hopefully help you avoid a mistake.

Fixed, variable or both?

Whether to fix your loan, in full or in part, is a major decision to make when taking out a mortgage.

Most lenders offer a choice between:

- **a variable interest rate**, which moves both with the Reserve Bank of Australia's movements in the official cash rate and as the lender determines, such as with their cost of funding or desire to attract and grow their customer base
- **a fixed interest rate**, which is locked in for a pre-agreed period of time. Fixed terms are generally available for one, two, three or five years, and the interest rate offered usually differs depending on how long it will be fixed for
- **a split loan**, where a portion of the loan is variable and the other portion is fixed. This could be a 50-50 split or some other proportion. A split loan allows borrowers to hedge their bets.

Naturally, there are pros and cons with each.

Variable rates expose you to the risk that they could go up, costing you more, but equally, they may go down and save you money.

A fixed rate provides you with certainty over what your repayments will be. However, there are sizable penalties for breaking fixed terms, including if you sell the property. These penalties are not as severe as they used to be but can still be costly. Furthermore, fixed rates typically block you from making additional repayments – such as if you come into an inheritance, windfall, sizeable pay rise or tax return.

Principal and interest vs interest only

Principal and interest (P&I) means repaying both the interest on the loan as well as the amount that you borrowed in the first place (the principal).

Interest only (IO) is pretty self-explanatory – your repayments only cover the interest charges, meaning you are not repaying the actual amount borrowed.

There are three main reasons why you would consider an IO loan:

1. **The loan is for an investment property.** This is because interest on investment properties is tax deductible.

2. **Cash flow constraints.** IO loans have lower repayments, so they can help you keep the property if you face a temporary period of financial hardship, like redundancy.

3. **Opportunity cost** (think back to Chapter 4). This is when the money that would be used to pay down the principal of your loan would actually make you greater returns if invested elsewhere. This is typically when interest rates are low.

When weighing up which option to go with, look beyond just the actual monthly repayments and consider the implications for your overall financial health.

IO loans typically have a higher interest rate than P&I, so they are not an exact like-for-like. They also often have limitations or penalties for making additional repayments.

Because you are not paying off the principal amount that you borrowed, IO loans will cost a lot more over time. So, if you use this option to help you buy your first property or keep your own home during a period of financial stress, you should consider switching to P&I as soon as you are able to.

Conversely, for investment properties, IO loans may assist with negative gearing, which can be lucrative depending on your personal tax situation.

Home loan vs investment loan

As mentioned above, interest only is more commonly used for investment loans. Yet there are other important differences when it comes to whether you have a home loan or an investment loan.

The primary difference is that home loans typically have a lower interest rate than investment loans. This is because investors are deemed to be at higher risk than owner-occupiers. When faced with financial difficulties, people are much more likely to sell an investment property at a loss than they are to do so with their own home. It is obvious when you think about it: we want to preserve a roof over our own heads first and foremost, and everything else comes a distant second.

There are also somewhat different conditions and eligibility criteria between them, making it important to consider factors such as your savings and investment plan, your age, repayment costs and your cash flow.

A crucial point to make here is that the loan you start out with may not be the right one for you in the future. Often, our usage of a property changes over time – whether that was actively planned for or results from a change in circumstances.

You may buy a property with a view to retiring there but rent it out in the meantime; turn your own home into an investment property when you move somewhere else; temporarily rent out your home while you go travelling for an extended period; or make a holiday home that you Airbnb/lease out short-term when you're not using it as your PPOR.

Any change in usage of the property can have implications for the type of loan that is most suitable. (It will also have tax implications, both for any rental income earned and CGT once you sell, so be sure to pay your accountant a visit, not just your lender.)

Offset account vs high-interest savings

An offset account allows you to link your everyday bank account with your mortgage. In doing so, the money sitting in your offset account is calculated against the balance owing on your loan, which reduces the amount of interest you are charged.

Say you have a $500,000 loan with a 6 per cent interest rate over 30 years. Your monthly repayments would be $2,997.75.

Now, take that exact same loan and add an offset account with, say, $5,000 in it. Your loan balance is now deemed to be $495,000. As such, your monthly repayments would be $2,968.78. That is a saving of $29 per month. Over 12 months, you would have paid $359.70 less in interest. That adds up to thousands of dollars in savings over the full 30-year term of the loan.

The more money you have in the offset account, the bigger the interest savings you make. So, if you transfer all your cash savings into the offset account and have your salary or wages paid into it, you'll pay even less in interest.

Another key point to make about offset accounts is that the money is tax-free.

The drawback of offset accounts is that they don't grow your savings. You aren't earning money on what is there; you are just reducing the amount of interest charged on what you borrowed. This is why some people forgo an offset account and instead put their savings into either a high-interest savings account or a term deposit.

Before rushing out to do this, though, consider the following:

- Interest paid to you in savings accounts and term deposits is considered income, so you will pay tax on it.
- Term deposits lock in your cash for a fixed period of time, meaning you can't access it early without being penalised.
- Term deposits are also interest only – the balance you put away doesn't really grow; it just has interest paid on top. In many cases, you may actually be going backwards because inflation means each dollar is worth relatively less, and the tax you pay reduces your total earnings.
- High-interest savings accounts typically only pay interest when you contribute a minimum amount each month, reducing your flexibility to do other things.
- To make financial sense, you would need to earn more in interest after tax than you would save on your loan repayments calculated using an offset account.

Ultimately, discipline is key. Even if something makes sense mathematically, you need to be disciplined to make it work. That means not withdrawing or overspending funds from the offset account, not redrawing on a line of credit, and contributing money regularly before the date at which interest calculations are made.

Demonstrating your ability to make repayments

When you apply for a loan, lenders typically take a broad view of your financial situation to determine how much you can afford to borrow and repay. This is called loan serviceability.

There are lots of things you can do to clean up your finances before you make a loan application that will serve to not only increase your chances of being granted a loan but also determine how much you are able to borrow:

- **Ensure you have a good credit history.** The federal government's Moneysmart website has information on how to check your credit score and where to get your credit report for free. If you find any inaccuracies, approach the report provider and/or the relevant organisation to update your report with the correct details.

- **Limit outstanding debts.** Money owed on credit cards and Buy Now, Pay Later apps reduces your borrowing power (while also costing a fortune in interest and penalties if you miss a repayment).

- **Credit card limits.** When assessing your ability to service a loan, lenders essentially assume you owe the full limit on your credit cards. Even if you never max it out, in theory, you could do so in the future, so lenders need to take this liability into account. You can improve your borrowing power by reducing your credit card limits and particularly by cancelling any cards you never use.

- **Show good repayment history.** Making repayments and paying bills on time is not just a good habit for yourself; it is also something lenders take a good look at before deciding whether to lend to you.

- **Review your direct debits.** These are convenient but difficult to keep track of. If you are paying for things you don't actually need, not only are you wasting money, but it inflates your expenses and reduces how much you can borrow.
- **Be diligent with your taxes.** Lenders will look at whether you owe the ATO money. Also, if you are overpaying tax or accruing penalties, you are needlessly wasting money and simultaneously reducing your borrowing power.
- **Live within your means.** Paying with cash and using budgeting apps can help you keep track of your spending and demonstrate your ability to manage your money, which lenders will look at favourably.

As a side point, if you find yourself unable to get a mortgage, you may be able to do a workaround by getting a private loan (which typically has a higher interest rate). Your preferred bank may then consider you later once you have demonstrated your ability to meet the loan repayments. Essentially, this is a trade-off between getting into the property market now with a higher-cost loan versus waiting until you can secure a mortgage with a better interest rate, by which time property prices may have risen further. Obviously, it is vital that you have a backup plan for the long term, just in case. Paying higher than normal interest rates for a long time is likely to be detrimental to your overall position, particularly if you run into trouble and the property market has fallen.

It's important to remember that while property typically increases in value over the long term, like any investment, it can also decrease in value.

Loan guarantors

If you're not in a position to get a mortgage in your own right, having a loan guarantor could help you get over the line. It is a strategy most commonly used by parents to help their adult children buy their first home or, in some cases, secure a business loan. (We will look at the Bank of Mum and Dad in more detail in Chapter 11.)

The guarantor offers the lender a guarantee that your loan will be repaid and provides an additional asset as collateral (often a caveat on their own property).

If you default on your loan (that is, you stop making repayments or fall too far behind to be able to catch up), the lender will seize ownership of the property from you and sell it to recover the debt. With a guarantee in place, the lender can do the same to the guarantor's property or asset that was used as collateral to cover any shortfall in the debt you owe (such as the property selling at a loss, missed repayments, any early exit penalties and unrealised future interest).

What this means in practice is that the risk of you not repaying your loan shifts from the lender to the loan guarantor.

Ideally, it may never come to that – you will meet your repayments, and the guarantee will never be called in. However, things can go wrong, with implications for everyone.

Loan guarantees can place significant stress on the relationship and can give the loan guarantor undue influence over your property and finances. Things get messy when relationships break down, as the lines of who owns and is responsible for what become blurred. The liability of a loan guarantee can impact the future investment plans and retirement options for the person who is acting as guarantor. In the worst-case scenario, both the borrower and the loan guarantor lose their respective homes.

If you do plan to pursue a loan guarantee, either as the borrower or going guarantor for someone else, it is ESSENTIAL that both of you get your own legal and financial advice beforehand to ensure you are fully informed of your rights and responsibilities and to implement strategies to manage the risks to yourself and your financial wellbeing.

It is also imperative that anyone involved in the loans has income protection and other insurances in place, as well as estate planning.

Beware of scams

It is getting harder and harder to be one step ahead of scammers. One of the latest scams is to send you an email that looks like it is from your real estate agent or conveyancing lawyer asking you to deposit significant funds into an account urgently, or you run the risk of losing the property you are purchasing. Buying a property can be a very emotional time and somewhat stressful process, especially in today's market where demand generally exceeds supply, making it easy to feel pressured into acting quickly. The scam works by sending what looks like a genuine email or letter but with a different BSB and account number. Be very careful to check all the details properly before transferring any money. Don't rely solely on websites, phone numbers, or online contact details – it might be one of those times when it's safer to confirm in person or over a trusted phone call, like in the old days. Australian banks are aware of these scams and will hopefully help you prevent a mistake.

Chapter summary

- Choose a lender that's right for your circumstances and aligns with your financial goals and needs.
- While interest rates are important, they're only part of the picture – a mortgage broker can help with this.
- Understand the different loan types, including fixed, variable, IO and P&I loans and what's best for you.
- Make sure you can afford the loan repayments, even if interest rates rise.
- Consider whether using a guarantor could help you secure a loan or reduce upfront costs.
- As with all areas of finance, be careful of scammers.

Chapter 7

Going solo or joining forces?

*"Get into the habit of asking yourself,
'Does this support the life I'm trying to create?'"*

Kristi Ling Spencer

In many ways, when it comes to property, what you buy isn't as important as who you buy it with.

Property (like most investments) should typically be held for the long term to extract maximum value. As such, you want its ownership to be stable and stress-free – not just when you first collect the keys but for as long as you have a financial interest in it.

Whether you buy alone or with someone else – and under what circumstances – will have huge implications for your planning and financing requirements, legal arrangements, responsibilities, estate planning and so on.

Everyone's experience with buying property is different, too: just because you or someone you are buying with may have purchased property before doesn't mean they have purchased property in the same way they are now looking to do with you. A recent divorcee might never have purchased property on their own before; an owner-occupier may never have bought an investment property before; intergenerational families may never have previously merged finances; an individual with a sprawling investment portfolio may never have bought a home for themselves and their family.

With that in mind, let's look at some of the quirks of buying alone versus buying with someone (and who that someone else could be).

Buying alone

There is no way to sugarcoat it: buying a property on your own is tough.

As an individual, you don't have the benefit of two incomes to save a deposit or service a mortgage. Depending on your salary, you may not be able to borrow as much on one income, which limits the type and number of properties you can look at buying. And you don't have what is called economies of scale – two people (usually) equals two incomes, but not necessarily double the costs. It doesn't cost twice as much to provide food, energy, rates, housing, etc. for two people, meaning living costs per person are lower than for an individual.

Having said that, it is not all bad news if you are single. The major benefit of buying property – or, indeed, buying any type of investment – by yourself is that you have full autonomy and control.

You don't have to negotiate and compromise to reach an agreement. You don't have to manage tensions and conflict – which is particularly evident in relationships where one person may naturally be a saver and the other inherently a spender. (Indeed, when this situation is not managed effectively, this is often the root cause of divorce and relationship breakdowns.) Having autonomy means you are free to make your own decisions: Where are YOU happy to live? What do YOU want to buy? What are YOUR values and YOUR needs?

Admittedly, it can be scary to navigate finances on your own, especially something as complex and expensive as buying a property. And it is a big commitment. But big commitments can bring big rewards. Plus, knowing you have a place of your own is an awesome feeling and goes a long way to helping you achieve financial independence.

Many people who buy a property solo are not first-time buyers, given the difficulty of saving that initial deposit on a single income. Rather, joint assets like the family home and/or investment properties have been sold after a divorce, and they are looking to purchase a new place to call home and start life afresh.

For those who did purchase their first property solo, often it was as a 'rentvestor' (think back to Chapter 5) rather than their own home.

Either way, it is crucial to have protections in place should you start a new relationship. Without a pre-nuptial agreement or similar contract in place, all assets can be considered joint assets for married and de facto couples. This includes ones you had before the relationship began, especially if your partner subsequently contributed towards them (such as contributing to mortgage repayments or assisting with renovations and maintenance).

Buying with someone else

Logically, buying property with someone else means you avoid the challenges associated with going it alone. Generally, you can afford to borrow more, have more than one income to meet the mortgage repayments and feel less daunted if the commitment isn't solely on your shoulders.

However, there are challenges here, too. Autonomy and control are no longer yours to enjoy. Decisions need to be mutually agreed upon, and different incomes, goals and values need to be aligned.

These complexities only increase as more people become involved. For example, you might be partnering with siblings or friends to invest together or pooling funds with your parents or adult children to buy a larger home to live in together.

Strategy becomes particularly important when multiple people are involved, as it helps minimise the chances of future disputes. Disagreements can not only damage the relationship but also lead to costly legal battles that can wipe out any financial gains you may have made. Strategies will also differ depending on whether you are cohabiting in the property or investing together.

One critical decision is how you structure ownership on the property's title deed as joint tenants or tenants in common, which has a major impact on what is called the 'right of survivorship' – that is, how the property is dealt with when one of you passes away.

Joint tenants legally have an equal share of the property as well as a right of survivorship, meaning the surviving owner or owners automatically inherit the deceased person's share.

Tenants in common, meanwhile, own a predetermined percentage of the property, which does not necessarily need to be a 50-50 split. These owners can also leave their share of the property to whoever they want in their will, which may not be the other property owners. This can lead to disputes if, for instance, the beneficiary wants to sell, but the other owner(s) don't, or vice versa. Another common dispute is where the surviving owner lives in the property and wants to stay, but the benefactor is their stepchild, who wants them to vacate in order to sell or turn the property into a rental. With a lot of 'second-time-around' marriages and children from previous relationships, there are many potential issues. If you walk away with only half the value of the property, can you afford to buy another smaller place? Do you want to? You may have to consider insurances to protect this. Other strategies include 'life interest', which is the ability to remain in the property until you pass. Each co-owner's estate planning should be clear on what their intentions are and ideally discussed and agreed with each other from the outset.

How you finance the property also comes into question. Having the mortgage in one person's name rather than all (which is separate from having each person's name on the property's title deed) can offer more flexibility for future borrowing, tax and investment requirements. An agreement should be reached and written down about who will contribute what, including:

- the deposit (whether that is cash or equity and whose it is)
- stamp duty and other purchasing costs
- loan repayments
- any improvements/renovations
- ongoing maintenance, insurances, council rates, etc.

These arrangements are typically more straightforward for couples since the property is generally a shared asset. For other people buying together, there may be more flexibility. For instance, if one person has higher savings or equity to draw on from another property/investment but the other has a higher income, it may make sense for the first person to contribute more or all of the deposit and the second person to pay more of the ongoing expenses, or alternatively to split the ownership percentages according to how much each person contributes.

Consider the differences in each person's situation and their broader financial affairs, not just those specific to the property. For example, first home buyer grants generally can't be used by multiple people on the same property – do one or more of you forfeit any entitlements? Does that matter in the grand scheme of things? At the other end of the spectrum, your PPOR is not taken into account when determining eligibility for the Age Pension, so retirees may be better off putting more of their savings into a property purchase to reduce the amount of assets considered under the pension's means test. But do you still have enough to live on, for holidays, repairs and cars? The pension is often not enough on its own.

Don't forget to discuss and agree on your exit strategy as part of your overall strategy. It should cover an array of scenarios beyond one of you dying. For instance, consider whether you plan to sell the property after a certain time or when it reaches a specific value. Think about what happens if either of you marries, divorces or separates, and whether either of you could afford to buy out the other if someone unexpectedly needs to sell. Consider if the property is being purchased for retirement income or if you plan to sell it at retirement to rely on the capital growth, keeping in mind whether a significant age difference between you might affect timing. Finally, think about how you would manage CGT if the property is an investment. Carefully planning for these possibilities upfront can help avoid misunderstandings and ensure smoother decision-making in the future.

The key point here is that when you buy with someone else, don't ever assume that your relationship and your respective circumstances will stay the same over time. Life happens, and things change, so plan accordingly to ensure you safeguard your financial interests, your relationship, and your own stress levels.

Potential partnerships

There really are no limits on who you can buy a property with. A partner or spouse is the most obvious and probably the most common scenario of joint property ownership. Yet, it is far from the only scenario.

Indeed, affordability constraints – especially for first-time buyers – and soaring rental prices in recent years are seeing more and more Australians look to creative means to get a foot on the property ladder. Pooling funds enables people to increase their borrowing power and break into the market where they otherwise would remain locked out.

Some of the buying partnerships I have seen people explore and enter into include the following scenarios.

Second-time-around without kids

Couples who are embarking on their second marriage or a significant long-term relationship that is not their first. Many parents will want some of their assets to go to their children from their previous relationship. Do you have other assets such as superannuation or other investments? Will your partner/spouse stay in the home if you have gone? Sometimes, the property is too big or too far away from family if the spouse is no longer alive, so changes may be needed. If so, the left hand and right hand need to work together. Planning needs to be made around insurances, superannuation (including nominations), investments, the home and the will to make sure everyone gets what they need.

It is complicated but more common than you think, and I have enjoyed working with many different types of clients to ensure this gets sorted so everyone can get on with living. There are solutions; you just need to ensure your financial adviser, estate planning specialist, and maybe your accountant (depending on complexity) are all on the same team regarding what is needed to ensure a smooth transition.

Second-time-around where one or both have kids with their ex-partner

Custody and living arrangements play a major role in property-buying decisions. The size and suitability of the property for children of different ages will determine your physical needs, while your budget – taking into account any parental support commitments, as well as each partner's settlement status and outcome – will dictate your borrowing power. The complexities are similar to those outlined earlier, but if you have obligations to young children, it is important that you have a plan to accommodate their needs. You'll want to limit challenges to your estate as much as possible to help prevent unnecessary financial and emotional strain and reduce conflicts that could have been avoided.

Case study – Bill

After Bill's relationship with his wife ended and some time had passed, he met Tracey. Very much in love and happy together, Bill and Tracey decided to buy a property with a mortgage and continue building their life together. Tragically, Bill suddenly became ill and passed away. When the estate was administered, it became clear that Bill had not updated his will or the beneficiaries of his superannuation. The superannuation, which also held the life insurance, was left to his children from his previous relationship. Tracey couldn't afford the mortgage on her own, so she lost the home and had to start again.

Intergenerational families buying together

Whether it is financial constraints, lifestyle needs or cultural factors (or perhaps a combination of all three), some generations of families will combine their finances to buy a property together. These options may include a duplex, split-level house, or a home with a granny flat (or space to build one). Such an option is popular not only from a financial perspective but also enables older people to maintain close relationships with their adult children and grandchildren, contribute to babysitting and child rearing, and receive care and support from their adult children as they age. If changes occur, such as relocation for work, having to maintain another property elsewhere, or family members needing their share for when they get married and set up a home themselves, this can be very complicated without a lot of planning.

Buying with one or more friends

Friends combining their resources to get into the market to purchase a house is not only an option for first home buyers but is increasingly used by older people (particularly women) who are divorced or widowed to avoid homelessness and the expensive rental market. Obviously, this requires a great deal of trust – I don't recommend making major financial decisions such as buying property with a little-known acquaintance or someone you cannot trust to manage financial and legal affairs responsibly.

You need to ensure a proper plan is in place that covers a range of scenarios, manages debt appropriately, and includes estate planning, insurances, etc.

Case study – Emily and Becky

Emily and her friend Becky had lived together as flatmates for about seven years. They decided to buy a property together because they knew they could live together well; they trusted each other and they both worked. We did some calculations to see what they could afford if they put in a similar deposit and paid the same rent as they were currently paying. We also looked at a stretch goal that was beyond the rent and factored in the extra costs you don't pay when renting, i.e. rates, repairs, renovations, insurances, etc.

We involved a mortgage broker and estate planner and underpinned their goal with the Five Foundations, specifically focusing on insurances. We discussed scenarios where one of them might enter a new relationship or face potential health challenges, ensuring these possibilities were accounted for in their planning.

They managed questions such as who gets the bigger room, who lives upstairs and downstairs, etc. Emily and Becky purchased successfully and were able to build on this, getting themselves a stake in the market, a roof over their head, and helping each other achieve their goals.

Buying with a sibling

Two or more siblings going in together on a property is more common than you probably realise. It could be first home buyers getting into the market together, jointly buying an investment property or holiday home, or even pooling resources to buy a property for an elderly parent with limited means to live on, which can then be leveraged longer term through its capital growth.

Case study – Nerida and Matthew

Nerida had been renting for many years. Her brother Matthew had a property but had moved back to where Nerida lived. Nerida had started a new career with good income and excess cash flow but no deposit. Matthew had a deposit from the sale of his property, but lifestyle choices meant he didn't have a lot to contribute to ongoing mortgage commitments. Between the two of them, they made an agreement that Matthew would pay a bigger deposit on his 50 per cent share and hold a smaller mortgage, and Nerida would pay a smaller deposit but pay a bigger portion of the mortgage, and they would extend the mortgage to cover some renovations. This originally made sense until the relationship soured within a short time, and a forced sale occurred. Now that the property had significantly increased in value, but the debt had not decreased much because the loan was still in its infancy, the perspective of who was entitled to what percentage became a nightmare.

Multi-generational living

As previously outlined, multi-generational living involves adult children and their parents – often retired or elderly – jointly buying a place to live together. This arrangement offers mutual financial and lifestyle benefits, such as shared living expenses, increased borrowing power, and the opportunity for closer family support.

Parents buying for children

Financially secure parents may choose to buy a property for their child to live in. This may be a temporary arrangement, such as 'Mick and Louise' buying a property for their son to live in while at university because it was cheaper than him renting, and he could remain there long term. Should things change, it could be sold – hopefully for capital gain in the future – or used as an investment or as a type of private rent-to-buy arrangement to help the child get into the property market.

Private investment syndicate

In some cases, family, friends, neighbours or colleagues join forces to create an investment portfolio together. This collaboration can be particularly appealing when focusing on property, as the high entry costs often make it challenging for individuals to invest alone. Alternatively, the syndicate might opt for a diversified portfolio covering a range of investment types to spread risk and maximise potential returns.

Chapter summary

- Sometimes, buying with someone else is the best or only way into property ownership.
- Remember that every situation is different.
- Try to cover all contingencies in your planning – particularly the exit strategy.

Chapter 8

Buying property as an investment

"Don't wait to buy real estate; buy real estate and wait."

T. Harv Eker

Hopefully by this point, you have already read Chapter 5, where we looked at some of the different types of property investments and the importance of identifying the 'why' that is driving your decision-making. If not, I recommend you go back and read it before continuing here.

In this chapter, I want to offer you a detailed look at property as an investment strategy. There is much more to it than buying a property and sitting back while it grows in value. (If that is what you are looking for, you may want to consider a term deposit or high-interest savings account instead.)

Being a successful property investor – that is, one who derives strong and sustainable financial returns from the real estate they own – actually requires a fair bit of work.

Even before you start looking at property listings and attending inspections, it is really important to develop an investment strategy that aligns with your goals, income, personal values and circumstances.

Your strategy also needs to align with the level of risk you are willing to take on. All investments carry a degree of risk, some more than others – you should be comfortable with the level of risk you take on, as well as implement effective strategies to minimise that risk. Never invest more than you can afford to lose. Make sure you put adequate protections and contingencies in place from the outset so that if the worst-case scenario does happen, you are not wiped out financially.

Enlist the help and expertise of your team here (your construction crew from Chapter 2). Collectively, they can help you develop a comprehensive investment strategy that is specifically tailored to your needs and goals while maximising your returns, minimising your tax liabilities and out-of-pocket expenses, and having your back just in case something goes wrong along the way.

Once you have your strategy, then you can look at what property to buy and how to manage it.

Choosing where to invest

'Location, location, location' is the mantra of every property investor. There are two aspects to location when investing in property:

1. **The big picture:** which state or territory will you invest in? A city or a regional area? Will you even look to invest in Australia or somewhere overseas? What taxes and incentives are available to investors there?

2. **The smaller, localised picture:** is the property within easy access to shops, schools, parks and public transport? Is it close to undesirable things like busy roads, high-tension power lines, industrial areas, etc? Is it in a desirable neighbourhood or an area with high crime rates?

Both are equally important to consider, so don't be tempted to prioritise one over the other. The small picture involves the nitty gritty details about who will be using the property, how large that pool of prospective tenants is likely to be, and how much they may be willing to pay for it. Meanwhile, the big picture will determine the various regulations and tax frameworks that apply to your investment.

Remember that while all property markets experience ups and downs over time, certain locations can be much riskier than others. A prime example of this is mining towns in Australia. Domain noted that some mining towns in Western Australia and Queensland had seen house prices soar by up to 30 per cent in the year to June 2024 as a mining boom pushed up demand for Australian minerals.

However, many of these markets had suffered significant falls at the end of the previous mining boom. For instance, Port Hedland had a median price of $810,000 at the end of March 2014. Twelve months later, that value had fallen to $685,000 – and kept falling. By the end of June 2018, prices had crashed to just $220,000.

This level of risk isn't lost on lenders either – some may not lend at all for properties in certain areas or require a larger deposit than they would for a property in a capital city.

Residential or commercial?

Residential property is the go-to for many property investors because it is more aligned with what they already know. However, it is not the only type of property that you could invest in.

When talking about commercial property, I don't mean giant factories, sprawling shopping centres and office skyscrapers – unless you have tens of millions of dollars to play with. To invest in those usually takes a more indirect approach, such as buying shares in listed property companies or Real Estate Investment Trusts (REITs), which are themselves a potentially viable investment option.

For everyday investors like you and me, I'm talking about buying a smaller neighbourhood commercial property. Think about a local corner store or service station site, a 'strip shop' on a town or suburb's main street, or a small office and warehouse unit within an industrial park. It may even be a converted residential property that is now zoned and leased by a commercial tenant (as is often the case for a doctor's or dentist's surgery, veterinary clinic, or daycare centre).

Investing in a commercial property enables you to diversify your risk and tap into different opportunities. The value and rents of commercial properties aren't necessarily tied to what is happening in the residential property market – people still need to buy essentials, get their teeth fixed, and have someone mind their kids during the working week, even when home values are slumping. Population growth in a particular area will increase the need for local shops and services, helping to drive commercial rents higher.

Older commercial properties can also be ripe for redevelopment, with developers seeking well-located properties with mixed-use zoning to construct multi-storey apartment buildings with street-level shops or offices. In some instances, this could deliver significantly better returns than could ever be achieved by leasing the property in its current state and for its current purpose.

Another benefit of commercial properties is that business tenants tend to be more stable and longer term. When we move house, we pay a removalist to move our things (or hire a truck and do it ourselves) and have our mail forwarded to our new address. Simple. (Even though it rarely feels that way while you're in the midst of it!)

For businesses, relocating to new premises is a much larger and more expensive process. Specialist movers may be required to dismantle and transport particular equipment, and the new location may need to be fitted out to meet the operational needs of the business. Additionally, there may be a loss of trade until the new site is up and running. Businesses must also encourage and support customers and staff to move to the new location, reducing the risk of them turning to competitors. Given all of these factors, companies tend to stay in one place unless relocation is absolutely essential to the ongoing survival and growth of their business.

Like everything, though, commercial property investments are not without their challenges. They may cost more to buy than a residential property in the same general area. It can also be more difficult to find a tenant, especially when the economy is not performing well – most of us have at some point seen shops sitting empty for weeks, months or even years, with the windows getting progressively dirtier and mail piling up under the door. The more niche a property is in its size, layout and location, the smaller the number of prospective tenants.

It can also be more difficult to secure a loan to buy a commercial property than a residential one. Because it is deemed to be a higher-risk investment than residential property, some lenders do not offer loans at all, while others may charge a higher interest rate and demand a larger deposit. Specialist insurance policies are also typically required, which may have different conditions and pricing structures than what you are used to on your own home and contents insurance.

Another point you will need to be aware of is that commercial lease agreements are quite different to residential ones – and more complex. Unlike residential agreements, commercial leases are typically for multiple years at a time, which could be three or five years for smaller properties or up to 10 years for larger ones. They also often include an 'option' for the lease to be renewed for a predetermined length of time. Commercial leases are also generally open to much more negotiation with a prospective tenant.

Finally, when perusing commercial listings, double-check that it is just the freehold property that is for sale. Sometimes, the business as a going concern, as well as the property it occupies, will be offered for sale together – meaning you could wind up with more than you bargained for!

Capital growth versus passive income

This is a big decision that will form the basis of your investment strategy. Are you more interested in the value of your property increasing over time so that you can sell for a tidy profit in the future? Or is regular income from rental payments your primary goal?

The former (capital growth) is typically where negative gearing comes into play. Negative gearing is when your investment is technically making a loss because the costs of owning and maintaining it are higher than the returns you are receiving from it. You can offset these investment losses against your personal income tax, which reduces your overall tax bill. The main goal is that over time, the value of that investment will grow and deliver you a nice after-tax profit once you eventually sell it.

The latter (passive income) can deliver more immediate financial returns. Instead of relying solely on the income you get from working to pay your bills and invest for the future, you create an additional source of income from your investment property in the form of rental payments from your tenants.

While it may be possible to achieve both simultaneously, typically, an investment property is better at delivering one or the other. For example, a rundown property may generate relatively low rental income, but the capital growth could be huge if the site is rezoned for higher-density development. Or a property may be really popular with tenants because of its location, which puts upward pressure on rents, but its value stays relatively static – which might be the case for properties that are designated for long-term compulsory acquisition by the government for a significant infrastructure project, scaring away prospective buyers.

Consider what is most important to you and look for properties that align with that goal. As part of your research on a property, look into why it leans one way or the other, as this will help you identify any hidden problems to be wary of or opportunities that could be exploited.

Ownership structure

Having looked at WHAT to invest in, the next step is to consider WHO will be the property's legal owner.

Depending on your personal circumstances and tax situation, it might make sense for the property to be in your name, your partner's name, or jointly owned – keeping in mind the difference between going on the title as joint tenants versus tenants in common (refer back to Chapter 7).

When buying a property with someone else, it's important to consider not just how ownership is structured now, but how it might affect you later, especially when it comes to tax. For example, some people choose to put the property in the name of the higher income earner to maximise tax deductions. While this approach can work well during ownership, it may create issues when selling. Capital Gains Tax (CGT) is calculated based on ownership percentages, so if 99 per cent of the property is in one person's name, they'll bear almost the entire CGT liability, instead of splitting it 50-50.

What works from a tax perspective now might not work as well at sale time, so it's always worth getting advice from a financial adviser and accountant BEFORE you purchase. They can help you weigh up the long-term implications and potentially avoid additional stamp duty in the future.

Alternatively, if you operate your own business (or, as previously discussed, you are flipping property through a company with its own ABN), it may make more financial sense and be more tax-effective for the business to own the property rather than you personally. However, this is a classic 'it depends' situation, and you definitely should seek advice. What makes sense in one season of life may not be appropriate in another season, so it's important to evaluate your options in the context of your current and future circumstances.

A family or other type of trust, if you have one, could be the best structure in which to purchase the property. Trusts allow you to spread the income and/or capital gain to the beneficiaries. Beneficiary situations can be different year to year, and what is appropriate for one year may be different the following year, but this allows flexibility and a way to stretch the overall wealth further by managing tax.

The same tax logic applies to self-managed super funds (SMSFs), which are legally able to own investment properties. The important caveat to note here is that all assets in superannuation are legally mandated to be set aside for retirement. That means you can't have your SMSF buy your own home or a holiday home that you will use – it must be purely for investment purposes. There are hefty penalties for doing the wrong thing in this respect. Some penalties can cause you to lose half the value of your fund!

The exception, though, is commercial property. If you are a business owner, you could use your SMSF to buy the property from which the business operates. That way, your super fund benefits from owning an investment property, and your business pays its usual rent to your super instead of to someone else. This is a lucrative option if the business is performing well. However, the risk is a potential double whammy: if the business collapses, your super may also take a hit from the property being vacant until a new tenant moves in and starts paying rent.

SMSFs can also become complex, particularly when they lack diversification and hold only property investments, as this can create liquidity challenges. For example, if the fund relies solely on rental income to cover a mortgage, and one of the members is in the retirement phase and wants to withdraw funds to support their retirement spending or buy a new car, liquidity could be a problem.

Investor costs

There is no one checklist of expenses that applies to every investment property. Each property is unique, as will be the costs associated with it, including but not limited to the initial purchase price.

For example, the size and age of a property will impact how much maintenance it requires. Properties in regional and remote areas can be more expensive to renovate or carry out essential repairs on, given the distance tradespeople must travel to reach it and bring in materials. Commercial or heritage properties may require specialist tradespeople to carry out works, which will typically cost more than standard tradies. Strata-titled properties will have ongoing strata fees to cover the maintenance of common areas and the building's sinking fund, which freehold properties do not have.

Then, there are the various management and compliance costs that come with owning an investment property. These typically include:

- a property manager to oversee tenant liaison, rent collection, rental inspections and general maintenance
- a buyer's agent, who you may enlist to help you find suitable properties in which to invest
- an SMSF specialist if you buy property using your superannuation
- insurances – it is worth exploring landlord insurance to cover against tenant damage, theft or vandalism that costs more than the bond will cover, as well as loss of rental income, liability and general building cover against damage or natural disaster
- selling costs like agent commissions and legal fees
- an accountant to prepare tax returns.

It is important to factor all of these costs into your investment strategy, as they will have a direct impact on your investment returns.

The tax factor

Tax is one of the biggest single considerations when it comes to investing, especially in property, because it alone can contribute to the difference between healthy returns or hefty losses. It also applies throughout the life cycle of property ownership.

At the very outset, stamp duty (also known as transfer duty) is levied on all property buyers. The rate of stamp duty is set by state and territory governments. Some currently offer discounts or do have exemptions in certain situations, such as for first home buyers or people buying new-build homes.

During the time that you own an investment property, negative gearing may be something you wish to leverage to offset your investment property costs (especially the mortgage interest) against your personal income tax.

Regardless of whether your property is positively or negatively geared, you will need to be diligent in claiming all legitimate tax deductions in full. Forgetting to claim deductions or under-claiming depreciation on improvements you make and new appliances you install means you are paying more tax than you need to.

When you decide to sell, CGT will be applied to any profit you make. If you haven't factored that cost in before you sell, you may find that your profit disappears before your eyes. There are some great strategies that may be appropriate to you, such as using superannuation catch-up legislation. It's worth meeting with a financial adviser to determine if this strategy is appropriate for your situation and to plan the timing and tax management of the sale effectively.

When investing in property through an SMSF or trust, its tax status, as well as that of any dividends you receive from it, will be another consideration.

Given this complexity and the degree to which tax will determine your investment returns (or losses), I strongly urge you to enlist the advice of your financial adviser and an accountant with experience in investment property matters like negative gearing, depreciation and CGT. They can help you to get the right structures in place and manage your taxes effectively over time.

Caution: Don't buy for yourself

What makes a good property investment isn't necessarily something you would like to live in or occupy yourself. You need to be thinking about it from a prospective tenant's point of view.

If you are buying into an area that is popular with young families, then walking access to schools and parks should be front of mind. You will also want to look at properties that are child-friendly, with easy access to the backyard, fully fenced yards, lots of storage space, etc. Young professionals, meanwhile, will typically want properties that are low maintenance with space to work from home and at least one off-street parking space. Students typically seek a share house within easy reach of their campus, so lots of bedrooms and good access to public transport are important.

Consider the lifestyles and particular needs of different types of tenants. For example, single parents may look risky on paper because they only have one income with which to pay their rent and kids who could damage the property. However, they may be reliable long-term tenants since they will want to provide a stable home for their children and remain close to their kids' school. Retirees may seem risky, given they no longer have paid work to generate income to pay rent, but without kids living there, they will likely take better care of the property.

Of course, these are generalisations, but the point is that there are two sides to every story, and you shouldn't necessarily rush to favour one type of tenant over another without first considering ALL of the various factors at work.

Chapter summary

- There are different types of investment property.
- Decide on your preferred return – passive income or capital growth.
- Buy using the right structure to manage tax effectively and optimise overall wealth.
- Understand the costs involved.
- An investment property is not your home – at least for now. Its main purpose is to generate income or growth, though some people move into theirs later as a long-term strategy.

Part IV
property in retirement

Chapter 9

Owners don't pay rent

"You are not buying a house, you are buying a lifestyle."

Anonymous

The fact that this book has an entire multi-chapter section dedicated specifically to property in retirement should serve as an indication of just how significant bricks and mortar are to being able to enjoy a comfortable, financially independent lifestyle once your days of full-time work come to an end.

It has long been known that owning your own home leads to better retirement outcomes. Not only is that because of the equity that has likely been built up over many years, which can then be harnessed for other things, but it often has a major bearing on the size of your disposable income once you stop working.

We touched earlier on analysis by *YourLifeChoices* that found that a self-funded retiree couple who own their home on average spend 13 per cent of their income on housing; for retiree couples on the Age Pension who rent, that figure balloons to 30 per cent of their income. Single renters need to shell out even more – 38 per cent of their income goes towards keeping a roof over their heads. Consider, too, that pensioners typically have less income than self-funded retirees, while singles are relying on just one income instead of two. In short, they are spending more on housing despite having less.

Clearly, this has a major impact on the quality of life you can expect in retirement. More money being eaten up by housing means less finances are available for other things – not just travel and hobbies but even essentials like food, clothing, and utilities.

Costs diverge over time

Another point to consider is how the costs of a mortgage versus the costs of rent change over time.

A typical mortgage for an owner-occupier covers a 30-year period. Interest rates will go up and down over that time, meaning that repayments fluctuate somewhat over the longer term. However, there is a fair degree of certainty over what those repayments will be from month to month over the full 30 years – they aren't going to soar or plummet in a single month. What's more, when paying principal and interest together, the amount of interest being charged gradually decreases over time as the principal balance reduces.

Meanwhile, rents are only fixed for the term of a lease, often the first 12 months for a residential property. After that, the rent is open to the rental market conditions of the day and, to a lesser extent, the physical condition of the property itself.

In Australia, the official interest rate, as set by the Reserve Bank, sat at 3 per cent in May 2009. It bumped up to 4.75 per cent for a period from 2010 to 2011 before steadily falling (reaching historic lows of 0.1 per cent during the COVID-19 pandemic). As of December 2024, it still has not reached that level again (though it came close at 4.35 per cent).

Compare that with rents over the same period. According to CoreLogic data, median weekly rents across Australia in May 2009 sat at around $325. By December 2023, that figure had cracked $601, almost doubling in less than 15 years. Much, though not all, of that increase has come since 2021.

What this all means in practical terms is that two people who moved into their current home back in 2009 – one as an owner-occupier with a mortgage, the other as a renter – face very different housing costs today. The owner-occupier's mortgage repayments are fairly similar to what they were when they first moved in. Meanwhile, the renter is paying almost twice as much. Save for a major windfall or hugely successful career progression; their income is unlikely to have also doubled over that time, so as well as paying more in dollar terms, they are also now having to contribute a bigger share of their income to pay the rent.

If (and yes, it is a big if) the same trends play out for the next 15 years, the differences would be starker still. The owner-occupier would continue to pay the same or lower repayments until the mortgage is completely paid off. The renter, however, would see rents double again.

When the owner-occupier makes their final mortgage repayment, it will be a similar size to their very first one. The renter paying that month's rent would be paying four times as much as their first rent payment. From here, their financial fortunes diverge even faster. After paying off the mortgage, the owner-occupier now finds their living expenses are greatly reduced, while the renter's living expenses will likely continue to climb.

There have been periods when rents remained flat for years, with some even decreasing, while landlords faced rising costs for insurance, maintenance and rates. The recent trend has seen a big adjustment to rents, but the costs of maintaining a property continue to increase. How this trend plays out over the long term is yet to be seen.

A homeowner does have costs to bear that a renter does not – council rates, the water connection levy and body corporate fees for community-title dwellings like apartments and villas. Nevertheless, these still typically work out to be far less than the cost of rent in the private rental market.

Housing and the Age Pension

An important point to note when it comes to the Age Pension is that your principal place of residence (PPOR) is not counted as an asset when calculating how much you will receive.

Currently, it is entirely possible to have a multi-million-dollar home and still be eligible for a pension. Indeed, in the most expensive areas of the country, such as parts of Sydney or the Byron Bay area, median property values sit in the multiple millions. (These values are typically based on the property's physical location, not the quality of the house that sits on it.)

However, being a homeowner reduces the allowable value of other assets you can hold to qualify for the pension, either partially or in full. This discrepancy is designed to help offset the additional costs of living faced by retirees who don't own their own home.

Services Australia considers a range of assets under the assets test, including:

- financial investments
- home contents, personal effects, vehicles, and other personal assets
- managed investments and superannuation
- real estate

- annuities, income streams and superannuation pensions
- shares
- gifting
- sole traders, partnerships, private trusts and private companies
- deceased estates.

In addition to the pension itself, renters may also be entitled to the Rent Assistance supplement. However, this payment has a fixed cap and typically works out to cover less than half of the rent, making it more of a small pension boost than blanket coverage of full rental costs.

Case study – Barry and Karen

Barry and Karen bought a property within a retirement setup where they own the value of the dwelling but don't own the land. Instead, they pay rent for the land and associated services. This allows them to get some rental assistance on top of their Age Pension and to retain more superannuation, as it wasn't needed to fund the initial purchase. Overall, this puts them in a stronger financial position. However, a potential long-term risk to consider is if they need to move into aged care and pay a bond, which is typically funded by selling the home. Since their property excludes land ownership, its value will likely be lower than that of a traditional home, potentially impacting their options.

Benefits of a part pension

Something else that many people don't realise is that eligibility for the Age Pension is not all-or-nothing. Pension payments can be calculated on a pro-rata basis, meaning you may be eligible for a part pension even if your assets make you ineligible for the full pension amount. Then, you top up this money with income from your superannuation to meet your actual living expenses.

The value of claiming a part pension, no matter how small it may be, is that it reduces how much income you need to draw down from your super. The less drawn down from super, the longer it will last.

Even as a part-pensioner, you are entitled to pensioner discounts and healthcare cards, giving you access to free healthcare and discounts on a wide range of other goods and services, further minimising how much you need to take from your super.

Word of caution on the assets test

You would think that, in a bid to boost their eligibility for a pension and the amount they can receive, most people would look for every opportunity to reduce the value of their assets to be assessed under the assets test. However, I often find the opposite is true.

Some assets, like superannuation balances and some financial investments, are fairly black and white in value. However, when it comes to physical assets such as personal belongings, household furniture and appliances, jewellery, artwork, vehicles and so on, people often overestimate their worth – perhaps because sentimentality clouds their judgement. In the case of appliances and computers in particular, these items retain very little value nowadays and are quickly usurped by newer models, so listing the replacement value or price paid brand new is a far cry from their actual value. In doing so, these overestimations can reduce the size of pension payments or deny access to a pension altogether.

As such, when it comes to the assets test as part of an application for the pension, be sure to use realistic market valuations and comparables for used goods in their current condition – because there is no point in diddling yourself out of a pension over such a simple and avoidable mistake!

One of the main reasons I wanted to write this book was to share strategies to help people stretch their money further and achieve a better lifestyle in retirement. With the right advice, this is often easier than people think.

Earlier, we discussed the importance of thinking holistically about finances rather than viewing them in silos, such as separating your mortgage, income, super and tax. If you work with a financial adviser, they can help you take a comprehensive approach, for example, by finding ways to reduce tax while growing your superannuation to pay off your loan. Consider speaking with a financial adviser about strategies like 'Transition to Retirement' to make the most of your financial situation.

Case study – Mary

Mary, a single woman in her 50s, worked with a financial adviser to create a holistic strategy for her retirement. By combining different aspects of her finances – her home ownership, superannuation and Age Pension – Mary was able to set herself up for a comfortable retirement.

By the time she retired, Mary owned her home outright and had saved $300,000 in superannuation. Her adviser explained that to meet the ASFA retirement standard for a modest lifestyle, she would need approximately $53,000 per year to live comfortably (excluding debt). With the Age Pension providing $30,000 annually, Mary needed to draw $23,000 a year from her superannuation to bridge the gap.

In her first year of retirement, Mary's $300,000 in super earned 5 per cent interest, generating $15,000. This meant she only needed to draw $8,000 from her super balance. The following year, her super balance decreased slightly to $292,000. At 5 per cent interest, it earned $14,600, so she needed to draw $8,400. Each year, the super balance reduced gradually as Mary drew down the funds she needed.

Markets fluctuate, and 5 per cent returns are not guaranteed, so it's important to manage expectations and adjust the strategy as needed. Mary's adviser emphasised the importance of continuing to build her superannuation balance while working. The more funds she had, the more flexibility she could enjoy in retirement, whether that meant purchasing a new car, making home renovations, or travelling overseas. This strategy gave Mary both financial security and the ability to make choices that suited her lifestyle.

Mortgages in retirement

In an ideal scenario, you would not have a mortgage in retirement. You keep working as long as you can and use that income to pay off the mortgage in full, then retire comfortably.

However, the reality is increasingly different.

As *The Sydney Morning Herald* noted in early 2024, 'Figures from Digital Data Analytics show that first home buyers in Sydney and Melbourne are in their mid-30s, on average. In 2004, they were in their mid-20s'. The same article highlighted that Australians are also buying their first home later in life, and typical mortgage terms over the same period had blown out from 20 to 30 years, 'with 35-year and even 40-year terms also available'.

So, what's causing this shift? Affordability constraints play a major role. Many argue that growing student debt from tertiary education is adding to the challenge. Young people are finding it harder to save the all-important deposit to enter the property market. In addition, the rapid run of interest rate rises by the Reserve Bank in 2022–2023 has made lending affordability tests more difficult to satisfy since these typically scrutinise a borrower's ability to meet repayments if the interest rate climbs another 2 to 3 per cent.

Back in 2004 and earlier, someone buying their first home in their mid-20s would easily have paid off a 20- or even 30-year loan term before retirement. Today's first home buyers, entering the market in their mid-30s, face the prospect of still having to make mortgage repayments in their mid-60s or even into their 70s.

COVID-19 also changed how many people approach life, with a greater focus on living in the 'now'. Some prioritise experiences, like travel or dining out, over saving for the future. Parents in strong financial positions often take their kids on overseas trips, setting high expectations for lifestyle standards. This lifestyle creep can make it difficult to adjust back to tighter budgets or the sacrifices required to pay off a mortgage, especially as retirement approaches.

There are multiple dangers associated with having a mortgage when you are retired. Loan repayments significantly eat into your retirement income, meaning you burn through your super-annuation faster. There is less equity available in the property to put towards retirement or assisted living if needed, or lifestyle luxuries like travel or a holiday home. Furthermore, the Age

Pension was never designed with a mortgage in mind – these retirees face the same elevated housing costs in retirement as renters but without the benefit of Rent Assistance.

Reverse mortgages

A reverse mortgage allows you to borrow against the equity in your home. Instead of making regular repayments, the interest accumulates over time, and the loan, along with the accrued interest, is repaid in full when you sell or move home or when your home is sold as part of your deceased estate after you pass away.

The appeal of a reverse mortgage is that it typically allows people aged 60 and over to access some of the equity they have built up in their home over many years without having to sell the property.

If that sounds too good to be true, then you are right – for many people, it is.

For a start, the interest rate on a reverse mortgage is often higher than a standard mortgage, in addition there are assorted fees and charges. There are also generally restrictions on how much and how little you can borrow. Depending on what you do with the money, you could delay or negate your ability to qualify for the Age Pension.

I also urge caution when it comes to reverse mortgages for the simple fact that you don't know how long you will live or what circumstance may throw at you in the future. If you live a really long life and remain in the same home, the interest on the reverse mortgage can grow significantly. What happens if the property market crashes and the equity you have no longer covers the debt? What if you pass away and leave your children or loved ones with a debt greater than the sum of your assets? The risks here are large, so the rewards of taking out such a loan need to be even greater to make it worthwhile.

There is also now a government scheme called the Home Equity Access Scheme. While the rate may be much less than that of an institution, there are more restrictions, eligibility criteria, and significant risks to consider. Like most things, you need to understand the details and get advice. Be careful!

Link between housing and health

Unfortunately, getting older increases the likelihood of adverse health conditions. Even with senior and pensioner healthcare cards as well as the National Disability Insurance Scheme (NDIS), there can still be substantial out-of-pocket expenses: things like support aids and equipment, specialist medical bills, supplements, any modifications to your home (e.g. the installation of ramps, handrails, widening of doorways for wheelchairs or walking aids, switching door knobs to handles for easier grip), home carers, and so on.

This increased spending on healthcare and health-related lifestyle needs is far easier to accommodate within your budget if you own your own home and have paid off the mortgage. For renters who must direct a big chunk of their retirement income towards housing, their remaining dollars and cents have to stretch a lot further.

For some, healthcare becomes a luxury when they are forced to choose between that or something as fundamental as putting food on the table or using air conditioning or heating to maintain a comfortable temperature during the extremes of summer and winter.

Furthermore, adverse health for you or your partner could render your current home unsuitable going forward – the most obvious being the need to avoid stairs. Particularly if the issue is sudden and unexpected, such as a hip replacement after a fall, you may be forced to find alternative accommodation and face moving costs that had not been budgeted for. Renters can be left temporarily stretched by having to pay a new bond and advanced rent at their new home before the bond from their previous one is released. Homeowners in the same situation may need to suddenly find money to cover sale expenses, such as any urgent maintenance issues, property styling, cleaners and gardeners, over and above moving costs. If purchasing a new property, they'll also face stamp duty and other buying costs, further adding to the financial burden.

Such effects can be compounded further if serious illness or injury occurs pre-retirement. Unexpected time off work or forced early retirement, especially if it is by the primary breadwinner, can throw even the most well-considered transition to retirement plan into chaos.

A major hit to household income at this stage could jeopardise your housing stability, particularly if you fall behind on rent or mortgage repayments. Homeowners may even be forced to sell their property earlier than planned and suffer a hit to the equity they had intended to use for their retirement. This risk is especially significant if it is during a market downturn or if a quick sale requires a heavily discounted price. This is where the value of insurances like income protection and permanent disability shine through.

However, if you have retired, like Mark, it is likely that insurances, such as income protection, are no longer relevant. Mark was living independently when he fell down the front stairs, seriously injuring himself physically and emotionally. Mark was so frightened to go down the stairs again that he became stuck in his own home, having as much delivered as possible but not able to venture outside. Health challenges as a single person can have a major impact, often forcing the sale of a property and a move to aged care or a more appropriate property – one without stairs, smaller in size, or with improved security and features. Eventually, Mark had to sell to regain his lifestyle, but the cost of selling, including stamp duty, ate into the value of his overall assets. This can drastically change a person's financial position, so getting on the front foot and making decisions earlier so you can get what you want may be wiser. For more on this, see Chapter 10 on downsizing.

Chapter summary

- Over time, a mortgage feels easier to manage as inflation makes the repayments smaller compared to rising incomes, while rent keeps going up, making owning a home a better long-term option.
- You can own your own home and still qualify for the Age Pension.
- Be cautious when considering taking out a reverse mortgage.
- Home ownership gives you peace of mind in retirement – less stress benefits your health.

Chapter 10

The do's and don'ts of downsizing

"Downsizing our lives is not a step back but a leap forward."

Erin Hybart

Before we dive in, keep in mind that some of the specifics around downsizing – like rules, regulations, or benefits – can change over time. What's true today might not be tomorrow, so it's always worth double-checking with a professional for the latest information.

Downsizing from the family home is a significant decision for many people, often marking a new chapter in life. It can be even more difficult and emotional to let go of your long-term home than it is to change your identity by letting go of your work and career to retire, given the familiarity and memories that have been built up within those walls over time.

It is also a decision that affects the entire family, not just the homeowner. Children and even grandchildren can have emotional attachments to the property they grew up in.

Uncertainty over where you will move next can create anxiety for everyone. Neighbourhood friendships will irrevocably change once you can no longer chat over the fence each day.

Once the decision to downsize has been made, the lengthy process of preparing the property for sale comes next. The longer you and your family have lived there, the more 'stuff' is likely to be packed into the property's cupboards, drawers, wardrobes, garages, garden shed, attic, and any under-house storage areas. Sorting through a lifetime of memories to declutter and pack up can be a hugely emotional task in its own right – daunting at the outset, nostalgic throughout as you uncover long-forgotten treasures, and a mixture of relief and sadness once the job is done.

It can be useful to involve loved ones, not just to share the workload but also to share the trip down memory lane and help to determine what to keep and what to say goodbye to.

Reasons to downsize

The driving factors behind a person or couple's decision to downsize are numerous and complex. They can be a blend of lifestyle, logistical and financial elements.

Perhaps the biggest one is to access equity, which we will cover in more detail below. Other reasons people look to downsize their home once they retire or in preparation for retirement include:

- having a smaller property that is easier to manage when the children have grown up and left home
- health considerations necessitate a lifestyle change, such as wheelchair access or a home free of stairs
- being closer to family

- reducing housing costs in retirement, especially where there is a large mortgage remaining
- paying off other debts
- a fresh start, particularly after a divorce or the death of a partner
- minimising risks – being less mobile in later years can make evacuation from fires or floods more difficult
- a change of scenery and pace, such as escaping the hustle and bustle of city life.

Ultimately, the decision to downsize is a deeply personal one that will depend on your unique circumstances, needs and aspirations for the future.

Unlocking equity from the family home

While I have said it before, it is worth repeating here: your principal place of residence (PPOR) is currently not taxed when you sell it. There is no Capital Gains Tax (CGT) applied, and any profit does not count towards your personal income tax – those proceeds are all yours.

If you have owned your home for many years – decades even – and paid off your mortgage, then we aren't talking loose change either. We are talking about a windfall of potentially hundreds of thousands, if not millions, of dollars. That kind of money hitting your bank account in one go unlocks a huge range of opportunities. If done in retirement, you also have the time available to go out and enjoy that cash!

There are, however, several major considerations about what to do with the money.

The do's and don'ts of downsizing

First of all, you still need somewhere to live. Given more restricted lending options for retirees, a good chunk of that money will need to go towards your next home, whether that is buying a new property, extended travel or entering some type of retirement living.

Secondly, remember that this windfall is typically a one-off. You are not likely to see a similar return on the sale of any other asset, particularly given they will all be taxed. And you are not likely to own your next home for the same amount of time to build up that level of equity again.

Finally, consider that while the sale proceeds from your home are tax-free, depending on where and how that money is invested, any earnings you make on that money from that moment is likely to be taxable. That includes bank interest accruing while the money is sitting there waiting to be used. This point often gets overlooked, especially by anyone who is unfamiliar with having a large sum of money sitting in their account (or at least outside of a mortgage offset account). Hence, before you sell up, it is a good idea to get professional advice about what to do with the money to ensure it is managed as tax-effectively as possible. Good planning allows many people to maximise their outcomes by avoiding mistakes and finding out strategies they don't know.

Pension impacts

Another commonly overlooked consideration with downsizing is how it will impact the size of your Age Pension payments and even your eligibility to claim it.

While the money is locked up in your home as equity, it is not included in the pension's asset test. As soon as you sell, you suddenly have a big lump of cash. That is usually assessable, although Centrelink may allow a grace period depending on your plans.

If you go on to buy another property using that money, it once again counts towards your PPOR and is no longer considered an assessable asset. However, depending on the timing, you might temporarily lose the pension between settling on your old home and moving into your new one. Once any grace period is exhausted, if there is one, any money left over will still count towards the asset test.

Downsizing home, upsizing super

One popular means of putting the released equity to good use after downsizing is to make a contribution to your superannuation.

As of 1 January 2023, anyone aged 55 years or over can transfer up to $300,000 from the sale or part-sale of their home as a non-concessional contribution into their super without breaching the standard contributions cap.

The downsizer super contribution rule was already in place for a number of years prior to this, but the age at which it applies has been progressively lowered – it had been open only to Australians aged 65 years and over from July 2018 and then 60 years and over from July 2022.

There are several conditions for eligibility, chief among them being that this can only be done once – so it's important to make it count. Other requirements include:

- You and/or your spouse must have owned the home for at least 10 years before its sale.
- The property must be a fixed home; caravans, mobile homes and houseboats are excluded.

- The home must be located within Australia, not overseas.
- The contribution must be made within 90 days of receiving the proceeds of the sale (usually at the date of settlement). In certain complex circumstances, the ATO may grant an extension, but you need to be proactive and seek the extension early to avoid potential issues.

The benefit of making the downsizer contribution is that this is a non-concessional contribution to superannuation, i.e. it is not taxed when it is contributed. Superannuation earnings are taxed at a lower rate of 15 per cent, which is generally much lower than many people's marginal tax rate. If you are in the pension phase (account-based pension, not the Age Pension), you may even enjoy a tax-free position on earnings, growth and withdrawals, ensuring more of your money stays with you rather than going to the government. Plus, not only does it boost the size of your retirement nest egg, but it also allows it to grow further when invested, providing more for you to live on in your golden years.

While the downsizer contribution does not count towards regular superannuation caps (limits), it does count towards the transfer balance cap. Remember that even in your super, this money will count towards the asset test for the Age Pension since super is an assessable asset. This is where advice can make a big difference. Decisions like who should receive the downsizer contribution, whether to split it between a couple or allocate it to one person, or whether to use it at all can significantly impact your financial situation.

Case study – Max and Antoinette

Max and Antoinette were retiring and decided to downsize to release funds to travel overseas. On their return, they wanted to buy a caravan, a new 4WD to become grey nomads, and a home more suitable for their long term lifestyle when they decided to settle back down. Max had been self-employed and had not paid himself superannuation in the leaner years. Antoinette had worked part-time and suffered from the gender pay gap, retirement gap and even what I call the 'career choice gap' (i.e. childcare workers, aged care workers, nurses, even hairdressers and teachers who have suffered from lower wages for undertaking such valuable roles), so her super was much lower than many. While they released a lot of equity from the home, they were still able to make non-concessional contributions to build their superannuation. As you can only use downsizer legislation once, this allows them to hold onto this strategy for the future should they make another change and meet the criteria at that time.

When to downsize

Deciding when to downsize is as important as deciding whether to downsize, and timing often ties into your broader financial strategy – particularly if you need funds for retirement.

As already outlined, you need to be at least 55 years old to be able to use the downsizer super contribution allowance, plus you can only use it once – even if you own several homes over your lifetime for longer than 10 years.

You will need to weigh up whether it is financially better to defer downsizing until after the mortgage is paid off or bring it forward to wipe out that debt. The latter will reduce the amount of interest you pay overall but will also reduce the amount of money you wind up with from the sale.

The do's and don'ts of downsizing

Carefully evaluate whether it makes more sense for you to downsize pre- or post-retirement. You may have more income while still working to pay for the costs of preparing and selling the property, but the trade-off is having less time to devote to decluttering and the actual move.

To extract maximum value from the property, you should look to time the sale to favourable selling conditions when the local property market is strong and there are numerous buyers looking around. Depending on your home's current state and the likely buyers, you may need to invest some money and/or time in dressing it up for sale – cosmetic work such as a fresh lick of paint, new blinds or carpets and some professional styling, or more substantial work such as updating the kitchen or bathroom. Your selling agent can help you determine how best to proceed here.

Don't forget to consider your own and your partner's health in your deliberations. Downsizing later in life, when you are frailer and may be suffering from ill health or even terminal illness, will be infinitely more stressful than when you are younger and more mobile.

Case study – Jenny

Jenny had not had financial advice for many years but had done her best to set herself up for retirement with several properties. However, all these properties still had debt. Debts still require repayments, and with other costs, her income did not cover the mortgages, which meant contributing from her own assets to meet these obligations. That was very hard when she was trying to fund retirement. Furthermore, Jenny was still carrying debt on her home loan, which was not tax deductible. Jenny wanted to retire as soon as possible, so there needed to be liquidity to provide for her retirement, i.e. to pay her a similar amount to her current salary without working. It was also important that she maintained her own home, as she didn't want to rent.

For Jenny, it made sense to hold onto as many of her investment assets as possible to support her long-term financial needs. Downsizing was the right move, helping her pay off non-tax-deductible debt and create liquid funds for retirement. This is not always the case; sometimes it makes sense to sell an investment property and use other strategies to dilute the CGT. It is imperative that you get advice BEFORE committing to any decisions, as it's important to ensure you're maximising your overall wealth. Centrelink opportunities can be part of this, but it's just one piece of the puzzle. If we had met Jenny earlier, we could have explored other strategies to put her in an even better financial position.

Case study – Nadine

Nadine's situation was quite different to Jenny's. At 70, Nadine only had her home and about $20,000 in super, having also experienced a 'career choice gap' and a divorce in her earlier years. She owned a beautiful home in the suburbs but wanted to be able to go to art galleries, cafés and theatres and experience the buzz closer to the city, where trains and buses were easy to catch, and she was also planning for any change to her health. While the Age Pension provided some support, it was not enough to cover Nadine's desired lifestyle. Fortunately, her suburban home was highly sought after by families looking to live near schools and sports facilities.

Nadine decided to sell her home and explore options that would balance her need for a comfortable place to live with her desire for financial freedom to travel, visit family in other cities, and enjoy new experiences. We looked at what would happen to the Age Pension if Nadine bought a unit near the city versus renting a property, including eligibility for rental assistance. We also looked at how cash flow worked under various scenarios and how best to invest her money – avoiding high risks while ensuring her savings wouldn't erode too quickly. In the end, Nadine chose to rent and enjoy her money now while her health allows it. This decision also enabled her to treat her children and grandchildren to shared holidays, something that wouldn't have been possible given their own mortgages. Nadine is now able to experience the joy of giving what would be an inheritance and enjoy this time with her loved ones.

Where to next?

Downsizing often draws your focus to the past – reflecting on what you're letting go of and the memories attached to it. However, don't forget that this process is an opportunity to look to the future as well, to embrace new lifestyle possibilities and revisit your bucket list with renewed freedom and resources. Do so with a healthy blend of excitement and logical reasoning to deliver the best financial outcomes since this process has a major bearing on your income and lifestyle for the remainder of your days.

A big part of the process is deciding where you will live once you leave your current home. This is not just an emotional or logistical exercise but will directly determine how much of the sale proceeds are reinvested for housing and how much is left over for other uses.

If you plan to purchase a new property, be aware that selling in a strong or rising market may mean that you are also buying in a strong market. Or, if you are looking at a major relocation, such as moving interstate, the two markets may not be at the same stage in the cycle. You could get caught out if, for instance, you sell in a falling market but buy into a very strong one – meaning you receive less money for the property you sell and have to fork out more for the one you buy.

In addition to the house price cycle, factor in whether you are moving to a cheaper or more expensive market. For instance, you will typically get a lot more bang for your buck if you sell in a capital city and buy somewhere regional or sell in a coastal area to move inland. But the opposite applies if you are doing the reverse. It is important to ensure you really want to live there, so test it out. Many people move and later realise they are too far away from what's important, and want to move back. However, selling a property in some areas can take time or fetch a lower price than expected, and buying again comes with its own set of challenges and costs. Remember, too, that you will have to pay stamp duty on any property you buy, which will probably be radically more than when you bought your current home. This is something to consider when people move to be close to their grandchildren, but then their children and grandchildren move somewhere else for work, and you have eroded some wealth.

Some people take the opportunity when downsizing to move to another country altogether, like Thailand, where housing is cheaper and the exchange rate works in their favour. International relocations to retire are very popular with Britons, who look to warmer climates in the likes of Spain, France and Italy. While

The do's and don'ts of downsizing

these locations may also be open to Australians, the tyranny of distance can be harder to navigate. Countries closer to us (save for New Zealand) also typically have a language barrier to navigate on top of their own unique rules, processes and pricing for buying property, particularly for foreigners, so factor in a reliable translator as part of your professional team.

Another popular option is to trade a fixed address for the life of a nomad. The equity released from selling your home could fund the purchase of a motorhome or caravan to hit the road and tour around Australia. Others move from cruise ship to cruise ship, where meals and cleaning are taken care of – potentially working out cheaper than renting and paying for food, a cleaner, electricity, water, etc.

Assisted living is yet another possibility, the need for which will depend on the age and health of you and your partner (if you have one). Retirement villages, over 55s complexes and aged care facilities have their own cost structures and eligibility constraints. There are differing degrees of ownership (are you an owner-occupier or essentially a tenant paying rent?) and varying levels of independence (some may include property maintenance, water, energy, and so on, while others leave everything under your control, which will impact your cost of living).

Case Study – Larry

Larry was thinking of downsizing from his home to an over 55s village. His main motivations were to be closer to transport – anticipating a time when he would no longer drive – and to enjoy a more sociable environment with easy access to shops and medical facilities. At first glance, the numbers seemed reasonable. The ongoing costs, such as insurance and rates, were similar to what Larry was already paying for his home, making it a breakeven scenario. The issue was the exit costs. There were fees on exit for any capital improvement, a general increase in the value of the property, and other penalties. The risk, however, was what might happen if his circumstances changed. If Larry met a new partner and decided to move, chose to relocate for another reason, or faced an unexpected need to sell, his overall wealth would take a significant hit. These exit fees could deplete his finances to the extent that purchasing a standalone property elsewhere would be out of reach. He might even need to draw heavily on his superannuation to bridge the gap, leaving him without the funds needed to maintain his desired lifestyle in retirement.

Larry's situation highlights the importance of understanding both the short- and long-term financial implications of downsizing decisions, especially when considering over-55s communities with complex fee structures.

A trend I've noticed among clients is buying the house next door as an alternative to aged care for parents or grandparents. It's a practical solution that seems to work really well for many families. Here are some of the benefits they've mentioned:

- It's much easier to check on Mum or Dad without having to drive 40 minutes each way.
- Parents or grandparents can live independently, but you're close enough to help if needed.
- The property becomes an investment for the future, either as a rental or for other family use.
- Families can use the extra space – like the garden – for practical things, such as parking a boat or creating more room for kids to play.

The do's and don'ts of downsizing

- Modifying the fence line makes it feel like one shared space, but still gives everyone privacy.
- It allows for a seamless, comfortable arrangement while avoiding the challenges of aged care facilities.

I also know of one family who bought a property, knocked it down, and built two duplexes – one for the husband's mother and one for the wife's mum. It worked perfectly for them, as it gave their parents secure housing while also providing rental income.

The dream versus the reality

Wherever and however you choose to move on after downsizing your home, it is important to consider the 'boomerang effect'. That is, if you don't enjoy your new home and new life, or your circumstances change, you may regret the decision and want to move back again.

For instance, an interstate move may not be all you thought it would be – isolation from friends and family weighs more heavily on you than the comfort you find in the different scenery or nicer climate. In particular, quality healthcare and specialists are generally less accessible in regional locations than in metropolitan areas. Sadly, it is not uncommon for people to escape city life only for their health to deteriorate or to be diagnosed with a chronic medical condition, with the necessary treatments pulling them back to a major city.

Yet, doing so can be very difficult and expensive. You may be locked out of that specific market altogether if property prices surge after you sell. This is especially the case if you leave a capital city, where prices are higher and generally grow faster than in regional areas. Depending on the amount of time that passes between when you downsized and when the longing to return sets in, you may have burned through a sizeable chunk of the sale proceeds, leaving limited funds to finance your return.

It may be wise to try things out before making a firm commitment: test out your desired new lifestyle and location to see if the dream really matches the reality. This could be renting a home in your idyllic location or renting a campervan or caravan for an extended holiday before buying your own.

If you do enjoy it and want to make it permanent, great! Proceed with your downsizing process and good luck. But if it turns out that things are not what you expected, you have tried out something new, created some new memories and still have your own home to come back to. Then, it is a question of going back to the drawing board to figure out what else may be worth a try or even if downsizing is the right option for you.

Tips for a smooth downsizing experience

- Start early and plan meticulously. The more prepared you are, the better.
- Make the most of the opportunity to declutter and start afresh. Be ruthless and consider holding a garage sale or using online platforms to sell unwanted items. The less you take, the more effective your downsizing will be (plus you will lower your moving costs, too).
- Research the property market thoroughly and choose a location that suits your lifestyle and needs.
- Understand the various expenses involved, including selling costs, stamp duty and moving expenses.

The do's and don'ts of downsizing

- Explore different retirement living options and choose one that aligns with your preferences and care needs.
- Seek professional advice: make friends with your financial adviser, accountant, and legal professional as well as relevant real estate agents.
- Consider the tax and pension implications of downsizing (again, armed with tailored advice from a professional).
- Take a look at whether you are eligible to use the downsizer superannuation contribution if it is in your best interests to do so.
- Prepare for the emotional and practical adjustments of moving to a smaller home.
- Focus on the positive aspects of downsizing, such as a simpler lifestyle, reduced financial burden and new opportunities.
- Don't rush! Take your time to make informed decisions and arrive at the best outcome for you.

Chapter summary

- Downsizing can improve your financial situation, but it's a big decision.
- Be aware of any potential impacts on the Age Pension.
- Consider your next move carefully.

Chapter 11

The Bank of Mum and Dad

"The bank of mum and dad is making the Australian dream of home ownership come true – for some."

The Guardian Australia

Chances are you have already heard of what is casually known as the 'Bank of Mum and Dad'. This term is used to describe financial and legal support provided by older (often retired) parents to their adult children to purchase a property – particularly their first property where the constraints to getting that first step on the property ladder are greatest.

In reality, financial support isn't restricted to coming from parents – it could be grandparents, aunts and uncles, older siblings or any other relation. Parents are simply the most common providers.

As housing affordability has worsened in recent years, the popularity of this source of finance has exploded. In late 2023, a survey by economists Jarden estimated the Bank of Mum and Dad to be worth over $2.7 billion, tapped into by as many as 15 per cent of mortgage borrowers. A separate poll by comparison site Finder published a month earlier suggested a slightly smaller but still sizeable 11 per cent of first home buyers received financial support from their parents towards their property purchase, receiving $56,231 on average.

The Bank of Mum and Dad can seem like the safest of options, both for lending and borrowing money. After all, you're family!

While there can be significant benefits to this form of financial assistance, it is not foolproof nor guaranteed to result in everyone living happily ever after. Relationships can come under strain, especially where large amounts of money are involved. Plus, what works for one or both sides today may not be the case in the future. Life happens and circumstances can and do change, often quickly.

Let's take a closer look at the various merits and drawbacks at play here, as well as strategies that can be implemented to help ensure the Bank of Mum and Dad works fairly and financially for everyone involved.

Types of assistance

The Bank of Mum and Dad has multiple tools at its fingertips to support those seeking assistance.

Contributions towards the deposit are perhaps the most common and obvious option. This money could be provided as a gift, particularly if it is tied to a major milestone – making it a wedding present or surprise to mark a milestone birthday. Alternatively, it could be offered as a loan, complete with a repayment schedule. Interest may or may not be added, depending on the circumstances of both sides.

A guarantee over the mortgage is another means of assistance. Under this scenario, parents (or whoever is providing the support) offer to guarantee repayment of the borrower's mortgage and use an asset of their own as collateral. This is typically used when someone wants to support the younger person's property aspirations but lacks the financial resources to do so.

Another option is for the Bank of Mum and Dad to buy the property themselves on their child's behalf or go in as a co-purchaser. The adult child lives in the property while the older generation uses the property as an investment, with the aim of pocketing the capital gain once it is eventually sold. Alternatively, a 'rent-to-buy' situation could be put in place, where the adult child pays rent, which is treated as loan repayments. Over time, they pay off the purchase price or refinance to a traditional lender once they are in a position to do so.

Whatever option is employed will ultimately depend on each party's unique financial situation and risk appetite, the strength of the relationship between everyone involved, and the value of the property in question.

Benefits

The goal of this strategy is to get younger generations into the market so they can enjoy all the benefits associated with property ownership (as we explored in Chapter 3). Any means of making that a reality can be seen as a win.

Having the support of parents or relatives can help younger people bring forward their purchase by several years, with enormous positive ramifications for their financial and even mental health. The earlier they own a property, the more time it has to grow in value. The faster equity accumulates, the sooner it can be drawn down and reinvested to compound their wealth. Depending on how markets move, every additional year spent saving up a deposit may mean losing out on tens of thousands of dollars in rent – money better used towards paying off their own mortgage instead of someone else's.

For the Bank of Mum and Dad, the benefits can extend beyond just the satisfaction of seeing their adult children become property owners.

With their adult children more financially independent in their own homes, living out of the nest and out of their parent's pocket, the older generation's finances are freed up for use toward their own wants (like more travel or a new car) and needs (boosting retirement income).

Additionally, giving financial assistance to adult children or relatives can be used as a means of bringing forward their inheritances, with the potential to reduce tax liabilities if those funds were surplus to requirements and offered little benefit to anyone other than the taxman.

Financial risks to the Bank of Mum and Dad

While the intentions of the Bank of Mum and Dad are generally good and noble, handing over large sums of money and/or entering binding legal guarantees and contracts are not without substantial risks – even where family is involved. Indeed, the fact that it is family involved can cloud judgements and lead to decisions being made with the heart instead of the head.

The biggest risk is that the Bank of Mum and Dad goes bust. Should first home buyers find they can't afford to retain the property, a forced sale occurs. They may be left worse off financially than before they purchased the property. Where do they turn for help? Back to the Bank of Mum and Dad, which may put an unsustainable strain on their finances. Worse still, if a loan guarantee was in place, the asset used as collateral may also be lost. If this was the family home, suddenly not just one but both generations could find themselves in serious trouble or homeless.

I have also seen a number of parents inadvertently give away more than they can afford. Typically, things looked all fine at the time when the arrangement was put in place. But then their circumstances changed – an unforeseen major expense cropped up, a natural disaster or health crisis came out of nowhere, and their investments took an unexpected hit. Suddenly, the money they gave away to their kids was desperately needed but no longer available.

Others look to sell assets in order to come up with the money to pass on to their children. This can be costly for several reasons:

- By selling assets and giving away the money there is less in the nest egg for retirement. What remains will be used up sooner, or sacrifices will have to be made in terms of lifestyle and spending to cover the shortfall.

- Selling investments will attract Capital Gains Tax (CGT) on the profits. Depending on the value of the asset in question, the length of time it has been owned, and in which financial year it is sold, that tax could be a painful pill to swallow.

- The right time for an adult child to purchase a property may not coincide with the best time for the Bank of Mum and Dad to sell an asset. If there is a market lull or the asset is sold on the cheap to access funds in a hurry, the returns have not been as lucrative as they otherwise could have been.

- Some people decide to downsize from their existing homes specifically to unlock their equity to use to assist their adult children in buying a property. Doing so reduces the amount of money that is available to purchase a new place to live, direct into superannuation as a downsizer contribution or otherwise reinvest for the future.

- There is also the risk of aged care, particularly if one parent is able to remain in the home. How will the aged care be funded? Do they have enough?

Where the Bank of Mum and Dad provides financial assistance as a loan, there is a risk that the borrowers are late or fall behind with their repayments. This, in turn, has flow-on implications since this money may be needed to pay bills or meet other commitments. If the Bank of Mum and Dad operates a business, the business cash flow could suffer as a result.

Another risk is the bizarre obsession some people have with claiming the Age Pension at any cost. The train of thought goes that by gifting adult children money – whether for purchasing a property or any other reason – you reduce the total value of your assets to be able to qualify for a full or part pension. There is merit in claiming the pension where you are eligible to do so because doing so means you draw down less from super or other investments to cover living expenses, making it last longer. The Age Pension – even the part pension – is very helpful for getting discounts on health, travel, rates, electricity, etc, so it is not to be taken lightly. However, the low value of the pension means it is unlikely to meet your living costs in full. Plus, claiming it sacrifices the control and freedom that comes from self-funding retirement.

Case study – John

John wanted to reduce the value of his assets to qualify for the Age Pension. His plan was to gift money to his children, believing it was the perfect solution.

What John hadn't considered was that he would be financially worse off by claiming the pension. The interest on the money from the sale of the assets outweighed the income from the Age Pension and invested more wisely could have generated even greater returns. The pension did not support his expenses, especially if unexpected costs arose or if he wanted to enjoy life's opportunities, like travelling or upgrading his car. Life is unpredictable, and protecting what you have allows you to adapt to changes, whether they're challenges or exciting new directions.

When I pointed this out to John, he could see how he could support his children and build overall wealth while keeping funds to be flexible for any future changes.

In the end, John decided not to give so much to his children at that time.

Elder abuse

Another unfortunate element that can arise when the Bank of Mum and Dad assists with a home deposit and/or loan guarantee is elder abuse. The World Health Organization (WHO) defines elder abuse as: "A single or repeated act, or lack of appropriate action, occurring within any relationship where there is an expectation of trust, which causes harm or distress to an older person. This type of violence constitutes a violation of human rights."

This abuse does not necessarily involve physical violence. Emotional abuse, manipulation, coercive control and financial abuse are also elements of elder abuse.

Specifically for the Bank of Mum and Dad, providing assistance in the form of money towards a property deposit or guarantee on a loan can lead to expectations of further financial assistance by the recipients. Worse still, recipients may resort to threats to default on a guaranteed loan or deny access to grandchildren unless more money is handed over or other demands – like changes to the parents' wills – are made.

Don't think that this couldn't happen to you. The Australian Institute of Health and Welfare estimates that one in six older Australians – around 598,000 individuals – are directly impacted by one or more forms of elder abuse. Most disturbingly, half of all perpetrators are a family member of the victim.

If you are experiencing elder abuse, or you suspect someone you know may be, speak up and get help to address the situation as soon as possible. Support and resources are available through the Elder Abuse Helpline on 1800 353 374 or on the Elder Abuse Action Australia website at www.eaaa.org.au.

Risks to the borrowers

While borrowing from the Bank of Mum and Dad provides the financial support needed to purchase a property, it comes with its own set of risks for the borrowers.

Sometimes the assistance comes with invisible strings attached. Comments along the lines of, 'You wouldn't have this house without me' could become commonplace during arguments or used to shame recipients into agreeing to unfair and unreasonable requests. Parents can also feel an undue sense of entitlement to dictate how their child's property is maintained or how finances in general are managed.

Alternatively, the strings may be plain to see but are agreed to anyway through a sense of obligation or from sheer desperation to get the keys to their own home. This could be unrealistic interest rates or repayment conditions on a loan or improper demands for access to and use of the property they purchase.

Another risk for borrowers comes not from relationship tensions but from financial constraints and life events. If the Bank of Mum and Dad unexpectedly needs to rescind an offer of support prior to a property purchase reaching settlement, the buyers would need to find some other means of completing the transaction or risk losing their entire deposit and the money spent on legal and other purchasing costs. Or they could already be living in the property when the call comes, meaning they are forced to refinance or sell.

In the example of buying under a 'rent-to-buy' type scenario, borrowers could find themselves suddenly homeless should the Bank of Mum and Dad be forced to sell the property or need to install a traditional tenant able to pay a higher rent.

Relationship tensions

Money is often the cause of relationship tensions; the more money involved, the greater the potential for conflicts to arise. There are many ways that the Bank of Mum and Dad could lead to relationship tensions – for either or both parties involved in the arrangement, as well as others who are not directly involved.

For example, from the time the subject is first raised, couples may disagree over how, and even if, to support their adult children's property ambitions. This complexity multiplies where stepchildren are involved.

Another source of tension may arise down the track in the event a relationship breaks down. If the Bank of Mum and Dad split up, how will a loan guarantee be maintained? Who will continue to receive any agreed loan repayments? If the borrower's marriage fails, how will matters be settled with the Bank of Mum and Dad (particularly if it is not their son or daughter who will be the one to retain ownership of the property)?

Then there is the question of fairness among siblings. Is it fair for one child to be gifted a deposit or provided with some other preferential support to get onto the property ladder when their siblings did not receive the same? If money is being provided as an advanced inheritance, how are matters adjusted to reflect the discrepancy – do gift recipients receive less in the will or nothing? Are all siblings to receive the same gifting? How does that work if one sibling doesn't buy for 10 more years and prices have increased and therefore deposits have increased?

The setup of the loan/gifting needs documentation and planning BEFORE you gift/loan the money to protect against pitfalls. The good news is there are ways to address this, often involving collaboration with your financial adviser, mortgage broker and estate planning/family lawyer.

Ensuring the arrangement works for everyone

The point of outlining the various risks above is not to scare you off embracing the Bank of Mum and Dad. Not by any means!

Rather, I want to empower you to make informed decisions. Armed with insights into what *could* go wrong and areas requiring attention that you may not have considered, you will be much better able to make plans and contingencies to mitigate these risks from the outset or explore alternative options that are more favourable for everyone involved.

Provisions and protections need to be put in place to cover any future increase in spending needs or hit to income levels – both for those providing the assistance and those receiving it.

This should be done at all stages of life regardless, but it becomes even more important when adult children take a chunk of savings or home equity out of the equation.

Both sides should also update their wills and estate planning to reflect the new situation. The Bank of Mum and Dad may need to adjust what each of their children will inherit to make things fair and equitable. Meanwhile, updating their will is essential for every new property owner. That may mean declaring any benefit the Bank of Mum and Dad are owed or entitled to receive from the property.

Some parents don't like the idea of making money in interest from their own children. However, they may not be in a financial position in the long term to gift them part or all of a property deposit. Only requiring repayment of the principal amount will dilute the value of that money over time thanks to inflation. A workaround that can suit both parties is to have the interest set at the inflation rate of the day. This means that the Bank of Mum and Dad is no better or worse off financially, while the borrowers typically pay a lower interest rate than they would on a traditional bank or personal loan.

More than anything else, though, you MUST put your agreement in writing and have it signed by all parties. It is easy to shrug this off, thinking, 'It'll be fine, they're family'. Don't forget, this is a financial contract with a lot of money and legal responsibility attached to it. As such, it should be appropriately documented, just like any other financial matter. This is to ensure that everyone is fully aware of and clear on what the agreement is, what is reasonably expected of everyone, and what the support being provided by the Bank of Mum and Dad actually entails. It also serves to prompt everyone to look at things from a logical perspective instead of an emotional one.

Specify whether any money being provided is a gift or a loan. If it is a loan, outline whether and how much interest is to be applied, when and how often repayments need to be made, and when the loan is expected to be repaid in full. Include contingency plans should the property be sold, someone's relationship breaks down, or a change in circumstances (like illness or redundancy) impacts the ability to meet repayments.

One final point: before agreeing to anything, consider whether the Bank of Mum and Dad is necessary in the first place. A mortgage broker may be able to find a workable lending solution for the borrowers. Alternatively, a creative approach (such as those outlined in Chapter 5 and Chapter 7) may provide an alternative means of getting into the property market. Don't let tunnel vision lock you into pursuing a particular path that may or may not be in your or your loved ones' best interests.

Chapter summary

- There has been an increasing reliance on the Bank of Mum and Dad as house prices keep rising and it's taking longer to save for a deposit and get on the property ladder.
- There are pros and cons for the lenders ('Mum and Dad') and the borrowers.
- You may need to review your will when deciding to help your kids into home ownership.

Part V

beyond property

Chapter 12

Once you're gone

"An inheritance is what you leave with people.
A legacy is what you leave in them."

Craig D. Lounsbrough

OK, I know... this chapter isn't exactly about saving the best for last. No one wants to think about when their time on this earth will come to an end. However, this chapter isn't about wants – it's about needs. Every adult NEEDS to have their estate planning in order and keep it up to date. This ensures your wishes are respected after you're gone and that your loved ones are suitably taken care of.

In terms of property, you are leaving a physical asset to a partner or other family members when you die. Consider, too, that this asset is not just numbers in a database – it is also someone's home. It might be the home you shared with your surviving partner or an adult child, the home of a tenant and their family, or the home of a business if it is a commercial property in question. Other people's lives and livelihoods are at stake here, so it is really important not to be dismissive about the process that kicks off once you pass away.

The reality is that much of what happens after you're gone depends on the plans and documentation you put in place (or don't) while you're still alive. In this way, their fate is very much in your hands.

Who gets what

As previously outlined in Chapter 7, whether you own a property as joint tenants or tenants in common has a direct bearing on where its ownership will go upon your death.

For joint tenants, the other owner or owners will automatically inherit your share of the property. For tenants in common, who inherits your share will come down to who you have specified in your will.

Leaving a share of a property to someone other than the surviving co-owner(s) is fraught with risk, given the enormous potential for disputes to arise. Co-owners will often want to retain ownership of the property to be able to maximise their investment in it and, as such, they may be reluctant to sell the property just because your beneficiary wants to access that money. They may also not be in a financial position to buy out your share.

Another important consideration is when a property is left to multiple beneficiaries. Often, this is the family home being left to adult children. Unlike shares or other divisible assets, a property cannot simply be divided. Beneficiaries must reach an agreement on whether to sell the property and divide the proceeds or retain joint ownership, which might involve treating the property as an investment and sharing the rental income. However, this assumes the executor of the will isn't forced to sell the property via a deceased estate auction to distribute funds or cover any outstanding debts you may have.

If the estate includes other assets, you may be able to trade your share of the property for a different asset. However, this approach can lead to complications, including disputes over valuations, potential CGT implications, etc.

Scenario: Second marriages

Disputes involving second marriages or de facto couples and adult children from previous relationships are among the saddest and most common issues I see in estate planning. A frequent scenario involves a couple who has lived together in a property for many years. When one partner dies (often unexpectedly and prematurely due to an accident, heart attack or late-diagnosed cancer), their share of the property passes to their adult children rather than the surviving partner.

In these cases, the surviving partner often wants to remain in the home, not only for financial and logistical reasons but also to maintain the memories and connection to the life they shared with their late partner. However, the adult children, whether due to poor relations with their step-parent or their own financial circumstances, may want to sell the property to access their share of the equity in it. This leads to a distressing and costly legal battle, with both sides grieving while navigating a lose-lose situation.

There are various approaches you can take to prevent your loved ones from facing disputes like those described above.

In the first instance, carefully consider whether being tenants in common is really the most suitable approach. While it may look more flexible on paper, this ownership structure can lead to unintended complications in the event of your death, as seen in the scenario outlined earlier.

You can also include provisions in your will and your property purchase agreement that give co-owners the first option to buy out the other's share. This approach provides surviving co-owners greater control over how to manage the property.

Naming the other owner(s) as beneficiaries in your will is another option. However, this may be open to legal challenges from other beneficiaries, depending on the circumstances.

One effective solution I have seen is to leverage your other assets to ensure everyone is provided for. Children from a previous relationship can be nominated as beneficiaries of your superannuation (ALWAYS make sure you have beneficiaries nominated within your super, as this is treated separately from your will), while your partner inherits your share of the home you shared together. That way, your partner is not suddenly left homeless while your children receive a financial inheritance without the weeks- or months-long delay of having to go through the process of a sale and settlement.

However, practical challenges must be addressed. For instance, the value of your superannuation may not match the value of your property, particularly if it has been depleted over time. In some cases, it might not be appropriate to leave certain assets to some people, and you may need to consider tax implications or structures designed to preserve ownership within the bloodline over the long term. These decisions need careful planning.

Ownership structure

Depending on the ownership structure, there may be other people or entities involved in the transfer of ownership and/or benefiting from the sale of the property upon your death.

A good example is intergenerational living arrangements, where multiple couples/family units have pooled resources to buy a larger property that they live in together. The adult children or other surviving relatives residing at the property may have multiple interests in the property:

- their own stake if they are co-owners
- inheritance of part or all of the deceased person's stake.

Other siblings or relatives who weren't part of the joint purchase will naturally feel left out if they aren't catered for in some other way.

Meanwhile, if you own property through a trust, company, or SMSF, separate legal processes will need to play out. That is because the separate entity is the legal owner of the property, not you as an individual.

Scenario: The granny flat

As Baby Boomers enter or approach retirement, a change in living arrangements is often on the cards. The demands of maintaining the family home are increasingly onerous and pointless without a full nest occupying it. A person's desire to travel and beef up their superannuation may drive the push to unlock equity built up in the property they have called home for many years. There is also more free time available to spend with family and watch the grandkids grow.

At the same time, their adult children are in the busiest and most expensive years of their life. Faced with mortgage stress and cost of living pressures, the need for dual incomes to make ends meet conflicts with the ability to care for children and manage school routines and extracurricular activities.

A practical and mutually beneficial solution that many families are adopting is building a humble granny flat. In this arrangement, the Boomers sell their home and use a portion of the proceeds to build a granny flat in the backyard of one of their adult children's properties. In doing so, they can also put a chunk of the sale proceeds into their super as a one-off downsizer contribution and still often have cash left over to support other activities. They can now enjoy being closer to family while still having their own space and independence.

For their adult child, the trade-off for a patch of lawn they would otherwise have to mow regularly is that they now have on-site support with household activities and childcare, combined with the ability to more readily offer support to their aging or elderly parents. Additionally, the new granny flat can add considerable value to their property.

However, these arrangements can become complicated when one of the parties dies. Because two couples/family units have a financial interest in the same property, things can get messy if there aren't clear, predetermined agreements on who is entitled to what.

If you and your family are exploring such an option, consider:

- Who actually pays for the granny flat? If the adult child funds the construction on their property, the added equity over time generally remains theirs. However, if the Boomer parents pay for the granny flat, will they get this money and a share of the equity back if the property is sold? Is this a gift or a loan – and if so, under what terms?

- How are the Boomer parents' other children treated in a way that is fair? Will they be given the equivalent sum of the cost of the granny flat towards their own mortgage/home improvements? Do they receive proportionately more in the will as a trade-off?

- What happens if either party wants or needs to sell after one of them dies (or for some other reason before that)?

Inheritance implications

Most people want to leave an inheritance as a legacy to support their families and future generations. Others may also want to acknowledge and contribute to the ongoing work of particular charities that mean something to them in the form of donations or endowments from their estate.

Deciding who gets what is only the first part of your job in determining what inheritances you will leave behind. Equally important is to consider how these inheritances will be divided and transferred to ensure the recipients reap maximum value from your generosity. Poorly planned inheritances could see your good intentions go awry and leave your beneficiaries financially worse off or see their benefits needlessly squandered.

First up is tax planning. While inheritances themselves are not taxed in Australia, any income or profit derived from them is taxable. This includes sale proceeds, rental income, share dividends or interest earned on cash savings. Your beneficiaries may be hit with a CGT bill when inherited assets, such as property, are sold or transferred into their name. For overseas assets, inheritance taxes may apply depending on the country where the asset is located.

Additionally, many people don't realise that income tax rates are much higher for under 18s than they are for adults. That means that if you leave considerable sums to a minor, the benefits may be eaten away by taxes. This is why trusts, specifically testamentary trusts, for children or grandchildren can be more favourable than direct inheritances or family trusts. Some people also use them to disperse those funds over time and in pre-set amounts rather than as lump sums that could be easily squandered by a cavalier 18-year-old.

There are even tax and financial implications for yourself while you are still alive. For example, in some cases, it can be better to disperse funds as gifts or loans to your beneficiaries before you die. Doing so can slightly reduce your asset pool to maintain access to the Age Pension or drop down an income tax bracket. The caveat here is that you don't give everything away and then find you have nothing to live on in your later years.

Then there is fairness between beneficiaries; a lopsided approach or blatant omissions leave your will open to be contested, whereas equal and reasonable divisions tend to be more difficult for people to successfully challenge. This can be particularly so among siblings or where a non-family member stands to benefit from a considerable portion of your estate.

Finally, consider the practicalities and wider financial implications of an inheritance on each of your beneficiaries. Inheriting a property may sound like a windfall, but what if that person cannot afford its upkeep, maintenance, council rates, etc? They may struggle to do so out of a sense of duty to you, bleeding their own savings until they are forced to sell, potentially at a loss. If it cannot be sold or rented out, they may be forced to live in it, even if it is unsuitable for them.

If one of your children lived in the property with you and the other did not, where would that child live if the property had to be sold? Would there be enough once the proceeds are split with their sibling to buy their own home?

Common inheritance mistakes

The problem with inheritance mistakes is that the person responsible never realises they made them – they are felt by everyone else once that person is gone.

Several mistakes in particular stand out for their ability to cause confusion, chaos and additional heartache for those who are left behind.

Mistake #1: Not planning

Ever heard the phrase 'failing to plan = planning to fail'?

Inheritances left to chance risk your wishes not being carried out. Individuals or charities you intended to support can inadvertently get overlooked. Disagreements between siblings and/or other beneficiaries are much more likely – particularly if you are divorced, separated or part of a blended family.

In extreme cases where there is no will and unidentified assets go unclaimed, the government becomes the biggest beneficiary.

Despite this, many people don't have the basics like a will. Figures are patchy, but various surveys and estimates have suggested anywhere between 40 and 70 per cent of Australians don't have a valid will. In 2023, the NSW Trustee and Guardian put the figure at 60 per cent of all adults in NSW.

Mistake #2: Failing to make updates

Having a will and your other estate planning affairs drawn up is one thing. However, it is a big mistake to think that is the end of the process.

As your circumstances change throughout your life (marriages, separations, kids, investments, deaths, inheritances, grandkids and, yes, property purchases and sales), your will should be updated to reflect these new realities.

Not doing so creates a lot of legal headaches and compounds the grief your loved ones are feeling. Who inherits assets that are not covered in your will? What happens when something has been left to a person who has already died? Do children or grandchildren born after your plans were drafted get anything? What happens when one of your beneficiaries has a marriage breakdown? Will your ex receive an unexpected windfall from you while your current partner receives nothing?

Sadly, I have seen these scenarios play out many times – and they could easily have been avoided with a valid will.

Mistake #3: When a will is a won't

Your last will and testament covers a lot of things, such as nominating your executor(s), dividing money and assets and outlining custodianship of and provisions for your children and pets.

Contrary to popular belief, though, a will DOES NOT cover everything.

Separate legal entities and certain financial assets are not covered by a will, including businesses, trusts and similar structures. Most significantly, this also applies to superannuation. Instead, you have to nominate your beneficiaries directly within those structures. Not doing so can lead to a drawn-out legal process, which will delay your loved ones being able to access those benefits and potentially cost them a lot in legal fees along the way.

Remember, too, what we have previously noted about property ownership: joint tenants have an automatic right of survivorship, regardless of what is in your will. Tenants in common do not have the same right, making it particularly important to declare who will inherit your share.

Mistake #4: Failing your surviving partner (if you have one)

Death inflicts enormous and often sudden changes onto a surviving spouse or partner.

On top of the emotional pain and grief, there are funeral costs, a sudden drop to just one income, and economies of scale disappear. If they aren't retired, they may need to take time off work – both to work through their grief and manage all the various legal, financial and administrative affairs. They may also be forced to move home.

Some of this is unavoidable. Grief is a natural emotion we experience after a loss. Transferring money and assets from a deceased person requires paperwork and proof of identity.

Yet, there are many steps you can take to simplify things for your spouse, which are often overlooked or delayed until it is too late. These could include life insurance and funeral cover, cash savings and an emergency fund, plans to meet any mortgage repayments without your income, provisions for any paid care requirements, and business continuity plans if you are self-employed.

Additionally, make sure to address any of the other common mistakes outlined here to ensure your spouse is as prepared as possible.

Mistake #5: DIY

Inheritance is a complex business that compounds with the number of assets and beneficiaries you have. Yet many people think they can save a few dollars by doing it themselves with one of those mail-order will kits. My advice: don't!

Too many people have suffered additional heartache and financial loss because these wills have been completed incorrectly, rendering them invalid. Even simple mistakes can leave them completely useless. On top of that, there is the growing risk of scams, which could result in you or your loved ones losing everything.

At the end of the day, you don't really know what you are getting if you aren't drawing up your will and other estate planning affairs with the help of a qualified lawyer and a practising financial adviser.

Case study – Isabelle

Isabelle's three children are now adults, each with unique circumstances. One daughter is married with children and also has stepchildren from a previous relationship. Her son has had a few relationships, but nothing has stuck just yet. Her third child, Jemima, is disabled and lives with her. Isabelle would like to leave her home and assets equally to her three children but wants Jemima to remain in the family home for life. This presents a challenge as the other two children have mortgages and will likely want their share of the inheritance to pay them off. Jemima, on the other hand, wouldn't be able to afford a mortgage. These challenges aren't insurmountable, but they require careful planning. It's crucial to start early, develop a clear plan, and educate all the children about how this arrangement will work. In my experience, when everyone is informed and expectations are addressed upfront, it's easier to create a plan that avoids mistakes, reduces emotional conflicts and issues, and ensures a smoother outcome for everyone involved.

Chapter summary

- Estate planning can be confronting and complex, but it is an essential part of your financial planning.
- Inheritance problems are many and varied – forewarned is forearmed.
- Ensure you get financial advice to help you with your decision-making process.

Afterword

Given that money plays such an important role in our lives, it is not surprising that there are lots of famous quotes about it. One of my favourites is attributed to the legendary Walt Disney: 'The way to get started is to quit talking and begin doing'.

You're not alone in dreaming of and talking about having a better life where you have the freedom to do the things you enjoy without the stress of worrying about where your next meal will come from or how to pay the next bill that comes in.

But even the best ideas are nothing without action.

I had two goals when it came to writing this book. Firstly, I wanted to provide you with some clear insights into the role that owning property can play in your financial independence. Why does it matter? What are the actual pros and cons involved? How does it affect retirement outcomes and quality of life?

Secondly, and perhaps more importantly, I wanted to offer some inspiration on how you can go about using those insights to achieve your own independence. How can you feasibly take a dream and turn it into reality? What are the various options available to you? What are the risks and benefits attached to each of them? What resources and expertise might you need to help you along the way?

Of course, there are plenty of insights and inspiration out there already – just jump on social media or turn on the TV. Sadly, most of this content is just noise. It comes from 'influencers' and self-appointed 'experts' with a vested interest in making money for themselves, not in supporting you to reach your financial goals and potential. Few have formal qualifications and accreditation behind them, nor do they have years of experience working one-on-one with individuals or couples like you to build and maintain customised financial strategies. Crucially, they may not have experience in helping someone rebuild their lives after a devastating loss – the death of a partner, a messy divorce, a natural disaster, a health crisis, a business failure or a vicious scam.

It is these experiences and examples garnered over many years being a financial adviser that I wanted to share with you in this book so that you could see first-hand what can and does happen in the real world and how you can use these insights to take action and improve your lot in life, no matter where you are currently starting from.

As we explored in this book, the affordability crisis of modern Australia means that many people now have to seek out creative ways to get and stay on the property ladder – often with the involvement of other people, such as the Bank of Mum and Dad, co-habiting/owning arrangements, intergenerational living, etc. Then there is the rise of rentvesting, commercial property versus residential investment, different ownership structures and so on. With greater complexity comes the risk of greater and more complex mistakes.

Having read this book, you now have the benefit of learning from the mistakes of other people so that you can avoid repeating them yourself. You have the knowledge to identify many of the common warning signs and hidden traps and how to navigate

Afterword

them accordingly. And you have a better understanding of just how crucial it is to start with a considered plan in place, not just to mitigate risks but also to maximise opportunities (such as legitimate ways to minimise your tax and amplify your earnings).

But, the key point I need to emphasise (again!) is that each person's circumstances are unique. The decisions you make over your property and financial affairs need to be made according to your own values, goals, needs, wants, resources, lifestyle and risk appetite – not anyone else's.

Just because someone (claims they) built a multi-million-dollar property portfolio from nothing or earned enough from their investments to quit working full-time doesn't mean your journey would be the same, that you have all their truth, or that replicating their approach would necessarily help you do the same. Compared to them, you are starting at a different time under different market conditions and different interest rate settings. Your income, debts, living costs, insurance protections, superannuation balance, assets and other resources will be different. So, too, will be your age, health, potentially your relationship status, family dynamics, living arrangements, and so on. It's like trying to compare apples with fried chicken.

Then there is the legitimacy of their claims – are they genuine, or is it all marketing spin?

This is why I devoted an entire chapter to exploring your 'Construction Crew' (Chapter 2). Who you seek advice from on your property and financial journey is just as important as where you do or don't put your money. If they aren't qualified or currently practising in that particular field, then they may not know everything there is to know about it – even if they are well-meaning, and that includes family or friends.

Finding professional advice

When seeking advice, a good place to start is the government's MoneySmart website (moneysmart.gov.au), which has a wealth of basic information and simple tools you can access for free, including a retirement planning calculator and budget planner. However, be cautious with calculators as they are not an exact science. They often assume a flat percentage return year on year, making it difficult to account for sequencing risk or changes in your personal income and expenses. Use these numbers as a guide, not as absolute truth.

It is also worth looking at the online safety section for advice on protecting yourself against scams and identity theft.

When it comes to getting tailored advice from a professional, you can seek recommendations from friends and family or local community groups – particularly those with similar backgrounds to you (perhaps self-employed, widows or divorcees, same-sex couples, single parents, etc). The relevant industry body is also a good place to look for registered practitioners in your local area. Alternatively, you could ask an existing adviser you have if they can recommend someone – for example, financial advisers and accountants often work closely together to provide their clients with holistic advice and can recommend someone who has the skills and experience in dealing with similar issues or circumstances to your own.

Be sure to review the relevant accreditation of any specialist before you visit them. For instance, financial advisers must have a current Australian Financial Services Licence (AFSL) registered with ASIC. A mortgage broker typically needs an Australian credit licence or to be authorised under a credit licensee (that typically means being listed as an authorised individual under a manager or senior colleague's licence). You can also check

Afterword

the ASIC Professional Registers Search to see if the person has a current and valid registration. The same goes for the Tax Practitioners Board (TPB) register to find a registered tax and BAS agent. Meanwhile, licences and registrations for real estate agents, builders and tradespeople are typically issued by state and territory Fair Trading bodies, which will have their own registration check tool on their website. Legal registrations can be checked through your relevant state or territory branch of the Law Society.

So, where to next?

Having said all I can within these pages, the next step is up to you. I sincerely hope you can take what you have learned here and put this into action to move yourself forward. Achieving financial independence and the lifestyle you deserve is entirely possible – so go for it!

And remember to be kind to yourself. Some of this journey won't happen overnight, but over time, if you stay committed, make wise choices, and if your goals are reasonable, you should hopefully achieve them.

You may like to join my mailing list, which is a monthly email newsletter featuring links to timely news articles, events, and reminders to help you stay up-to-date and on track. Simply send your details to hello@onyourowntwofeet.com.au

Finally, my door is always open (I love meeting new people!) so feel free to contact me any time or reach out on email, Facebook, Instagram or LinkedIn – my details are overleaf.

Wishing you the best of health, wealth and happiness,

Helen

About the author

Helen Baker is a highly credentialled, award-winning and seasoned finance expert. She is a conference speaker, the author of several books, an international philanthropist and the founder of On Your Own Two Feet, an Australia-wide service dedicated to empowering women to gain and retain their financial freedom. Helen is a sought-after expert finance commentator and contributor in TV and print media, and is dedicated to improving all women's financial literacy.

🌐 onyourowntwofeet.com.au
@ hello@onyourowntwofeet.com.au
📘 onyourown2feet
🔗 helenbaker2
📷 onyourowntwofeet

References

Chapter 1. Essential financial foundations

Insurance Council of Australia 2023, 'ICA Statement – 19 August 2023', insurancecouncil.com.au/resource/ica-statement-19-august-2023

Australian Bureau of Statistics 2023, 'Life expectancy', abs.gov.au/statistics/people/population/life-expectancy/latest-release

Workplace Gender Equality Agency 2024, 'Promoting and improving gender equality in the workplace', wgea.gov.au/

Australian Taxation Office 2024, 'Self-managed super fund quarterly statistical report – March 2024',

ato.gov.au/individuals-and-families/super-for-individuals-and-families/self-managed-super-funds-smsf/in-detail/statistics/quarterly-reports/2024/self-managed-super-fund-quarterly-statistical-report-march-2024

Jamie Hersch 2022, 'If you don't, who will? 12 million Australians have no estate plans', Finder, finder.com.au/news/australians-have-no-estate-plans

Chapter 3. Advantages of owning your own home

Adviser Voice 2024, 'Household wealth rises to record over $16 trillion, spurred on by property', adviservoice.com.au/2024/06/household-wealth-rises-to-record-over-16-trillion-spurred-on-by-property

Australian Bureau of Statistics 2022, 'Housing Occupancy and Costs', abs.gov.au/statistics/people/housing/housing-occupancy-and-costs/2019-20

Australian Institute of Health and Welfare 2024, 'Home ownership and housing tenure', aihw.gov.au/reports/australias-welfare/home-ownership-and-housing-tenure

Australian Bureau of Statistics 2023, 'Estimating Homelessness: Census', abs.gov.au/statistics/people/housing/estimating-homelessness-census/2021

Australian Human Rights Commission 2019, 'Risk of Homelessness in Older Women', humanrights.gov.au/our-work/age-discrimination/projects/risk-homelessness-older-women

Matt Grudnoff 2024, 'Retirement Affordability Index: inflation falls hardest on those who can least afford it', YourLifeChoices, yourlifechoices.com.au/retirement-affordability-index/retirement-affordability-index-aug-24/

Live Like Her Challenge 2024, livelikeherchallenge.com.au/cms/about

Chapter 4. The opportunity cost

Australian Taxation Office 2024, 'Study and training loan indexation rates', ato.gov.au/tax-rates-and-codes/study-and-training-support-loans-indexation-rates

Money Smart 2024, 'Tax and super', moneysmart.gov.au/how-super-works/tax-and-super

Australian Taxation Office 2023, 'Super co-contribution', ato.gov.au/individuals-and-families/super-for-individuals-and-families/super/growing-and-keeping-track-of-your-super/how-to-save-more-in-your-super/government-super-contributions/super-co-contribution

References

The Australia Institute's Centre for Future Work 2023, 'A Better Future for Self-Employment: How is it changing, and how can 'gig' work be regulated?', futurework.org.au/wp-content/uploads/sites/2/2023/12/Self-employment-myths-and-realities-FINAL-2.pdf

Forbes 2024, 'Mike Cannon-Brookes', forbes.com/profile/mike-cannon-brookes/

Forbes 2024, 'Scott Farquhar', forbes.com/profile/scott-farquhar/

Bing Lee 2024, 'About Us', binglee.com.au/articles/about-us

Haigh's Chocolates 2024, 'Our History', haighschocolates.com.au/our-history

Ray White 2024, 'Family History', raywhite.com/about-us/history

Chapter 5. To occupy or to lease?

Australian Taxation Office 2024, 'First home super saver scheme', ato.gov.au/individuals-and-families/super-for-individuals-and-families/super/withdrawing-and-using-your-super/early-access-to-super/first-home-super-saver-scheme

Brett Warren 2024, 'How many Australians own an investment property?', Property Update, propertyupdate.com.au/how-many-australians-own-an-investment-property

Reserve Bank of Australia 2017, 'Box B: Households' Investment Property Exposures: Insights from Tax Data', rba.gov.au/publications/fsr/2017/oct/box-b

Australian Taxation Office 2020, 'Renovating properties', www.ato.gov.au/businesses-and-organisations/assets-and-property/property/property-development-building-and-renovating/renovating-properties

Rachel Clayton 2022, 'Thousands of people with side businesses could have the wrong home insurance, experts say', ABC News, abc.net.au/news/2022-07-20/side-businesses-voiding-home-insurance-widespread/101246862

Chapter 6. Navigating property finance

Belinda Williamson 2024, 'Compare the big 4 banks in Australia', Canstar, canstar.com.au/home-loans/compare-the-big-four-banks-in-australia

Moneysmart 2024, 'Credit scores and credit reports', moneysmart.gov.au/managing-debt/credit-scores-and-credit-reports

Chapter 7. Going solo or joining forces?

Australian Taxation Office 2024, 'Co-ownership and right of survivorship', ato.gov.au/individuals-and-families/investments-and-assets/capital-gains-tax/inherited-assets-and-capital-gains-tax/inherited-property-and-cgt/co-ownership-and-right-of-survivorship

Chapter 8. Buying property as an investment

Jessica Taulaga 2024, 'How the boom and bust of the mining industry affects the housing market in nearby regional towns', Domain, domain.com.au/news/are-mining-regions-in-a-property-bubble-of-their-own

Chapter 9. Owners don't pay rent

Helen Baker 2024, 'What inflation means for your retirement outlook', YourLifeChoices, yourlifechoices.com.au/retirement-affordability-index/what-inflation-means-for-your-retirement-planning

Reserve Bank of Australia 2024, 'Cash Rate Target', rba.gov.au/statistics/cash-rate

CoreLogic 2024, 'Australia's median rent hits new record, surpasses $600 per week', corelogic.com.au/news-research/news/2024/australias-median-rent-hits-new-record,-surpasses-$600-per-week

Services Australia 2024, 'Assets test', servicesaustralia.gov.au/assets-test-for-age-pension

References

Services Australia 2024, 'Asset types', servicesaustralia.gov.au/asset-types

Services Australia 2024, 'How much you can get', servicesaustralia.gov.au/how-much-rent-assistance-you-can-get

John Collett 2024, 'As houses get more expensive, first home buyers are getting older', *The Sydney Morning Herald*, smh.com.au/money/borrowing/as-houses-get-more-expensive-first-home-buyers-are-getting-older-20240215-p5f57b

Chapter 10. The do's and don'ts of downsizing

Australian Taxation Office 2024, 'Downsizer super contributions', ato.gov.au/individuals-and-families/super-for-individuals-and-families/super/growing-and-keeping-track-of-your-super/how-to-save-more-in-your-super/downsizer-super-contributions

Chapter 11. The Bank of Mum and Dad

Hannah Wootton 2023, 'How much money are parents lending kids to buy houses now? Take a look, *The Australian Financial Review*, afr.com/companies/financial-services/the-bank-of-mum-and-dad-is-good-for-70-000-new-analysis-concludes-20231129-p5enpp

Tamika Seeto 2023, 'First-home buyers reveal huge amount Aussie parents gifted them', Yahoo! Finance, au.finance.yahoo.com/news/first-home-buyers-reveal-huge-amount-aussie-parents-gifted-them-201221909.html

World Health Organization 2024, 'Abuse of older people', who.int/news-room/fact-sheets/detail/abuse-of-older-people

Australian Institute of Health and Welfare 2024, 'Older people', aihw.gov.au/family-domestic-and-sexual-violence/population-groups/older-people#abuse

Chapter 12. Once you're gone

NSW Government 2024, 'Are you one of the 60% of people in NSW without a legal Will?', nsw.gov.au/departments-and-agencies/trustee-guardian/news-stories/are-you-one-of-60-of-people-nsw-without-a-legal-will

Afterword

MoneySmart 2025, 'Retirement planner', moneysmart.gov.au/retirement-income/retirement-planner

MoneySmart 2025, 'Budget planner', moneysmart.gov.au/budgeting/budget-planner

MoneySmart 2025, 'Online safety', moneysmart.gov.au/online-safety

ASIC Professional Registers Search 2025, service.asic.gov.au/search

Tax Practitioners Board 2025, 'Finding and using a tax practitioner', tpb.gov.au/finding-and-using-tax-practitioner